The Occasional Vegetarian

Elaine Louie

The Occasional Vegetarian

100 Delicious Dishes That Put Vegetables
at the Center of the Plate

 HYPERION

New York

Library of Congress Cataloging-in-Publication Data

Louie, Elaine.
   The occasional vegetarian : 100 delicious dishes that put vegetables at the
center of the plate / Elaine Louie.
      p.   cm.
   ISBN: 978-1-4013-1036-3
   1. Vegetarian cooking.   2. Cookbooks.   I. Title.
   TX837.L645 2011
   641.5'636—dc22

                                                                    2011001620

Hyperion books are available for special promotions and premiums.
For details contact the HarperCollins Special Markets Department in the
New York office at 212-207-7528, fax 212-207-7222, or email spsales@harpercollins.com.

Book design by Karen Minster

FIRST EDITION

10   9   8   7   6   5   4   3   2   1

SUSTAINABLE FORESTRY INITIATIVE · Certified Fiber Sourcing · www.sfiprogram.org

THIS LABEL APPLIES TO TEXT STOCK

We try to produce the most beautiful books possible, and we are also extremely
concerned about the impact of our manufacturing process on the forests of the world
and the environment as a whole. Accordingly, we've made sure that all of the paper we use
has been certified as coming from forests that are managed, to ensure the protection
of the people and wildlife dependent upon them.

For Anna

Contents

C

E

G

H

L

M

N

for Noodles and Pastas

Foreword

by Pete Wells **Dining Editor,** *The New York Times*

Vegetarians were once an orthodox group, but in recent years their tribe has become rife with heresies and schisms. Most controversial are the occasional vegetarians, and there are many of them nowadays. Some are convinced that they will live longer if they eat somewhat less meat. Others are reformed carnivores who claim to be trying to give up meat altogether, but still backslide from time to time. Often it is the aroma of frying bacon that leads them astray from the path of righteousness. Then there are the mixed marriages: a devotee of charcuterie who marries a vegan. At home he is chaste; when he is away from his wife and out on the road, lock up your rillettes.

You can condemn these pilgrims adrift in the land of the meatless, or you can forgive them. Either way, you might as well put something on the stove, because they're going to be hungry again come dinnertime. No matter what kind of eater you are, you ought to get a thrill when vegetables are on the table. Elaine Louie is no vegetarian, but she swoons when she comes across a really delicious meatless recipe. Sometimes she swoons so much that she starts to talk about how good the dish would taste with a little ham thrown in. But like most of us, she tries to keep the faith. When food tastes great, after all, everybody's a believer.

The Occasional Vegetarian

Introduction

The *Occasional Vegetarian* is an ode to vegetables, to their beauty, their versatility, and their ability not just to delight us, but also to fill and satisfy us. Other writers, especially Michael Pollan, have written about the dilemmas of eating meat or not. There are dozens, if not hundreds, of books that explore the benefits of vegetarianism.

This book is a celebration of vegetarian dishes, of the seasons, and of the Union Square Greenmarket in Manhattan. The dishes come from more than ninety chefs, cookbook authors, and talented home cooks, and all of the recipes are designed for the home cook.

Nearly all of the chefs and cooks buy much of their produce from local purveyors, many of whom are at the Greenmarket. There, throughout the year, the vegetables (and fruits) beckon. In spring, there are asparagus, big, fat, and fleshy, and some that are pencil thin. In July, the corn begins to show up, sweet, tender, and best cooked in no more than three minutes. One of the most popular farmers said, "Three minutes? I cook it in two." Sometimes, he said, he just eats it raw. As people pick their corn, they usually fall into three different camps: eaters of white, yellow, or bicolor corn. I just ask which is the sweetest that day, and whatever the farmer answers, I buy.

Come August, the tomatoes, bright red ones straight from the fields of New Jersey, and an array of heirloom species make their debut. Each year, the variety of heirloom tomatoes seems to increase: pink ones, green ones, purple ones, orange ones. Windfall Farms sells the tiny, dime-sized, intensely sweet Matt's Wild Cherry on the vines. Other farms have the deeply flavored, tender, red Brandywine, which should be eaten soon after bringing it home or its skin begins to split.

In the fall, the squashes arrive, the perennially popular curvy, hourglass-figured butternut, whose color gives new meaning to the word *beige*, and the yellow delicata, striped in green. Autumn is also the time of mushrooms, the foraged kind including chanterelles and hen of the woods, and the cultivated ones like cremini, shiitake, and the great ruffly oysters. Potatoes abound: fingerlings, Yukons, russets, and the aptly named purple Peruvians, whose skin and flesh are indeed purple. There are brussels sprouts on the stem, and cabbages ranging from pale green to dark green to purple. There are mounds of apples as well. The Honeycrisp, which does not lose its shape and turn into applesauce when cooked, makes its appearance in two vegetable dishes in this book: nestled alongside brussels sprouts in Carmen Quagliata's recipe for Roasted Brussels Sprouts, Butternut Squash, and Apple with Candied Walnuts or tucked beneath cabbage in Didier Elena's recipe for Fall Vegetable Cookpot: Braised Red and Green Cabbage.

In this book, vegetables are whipped into flans, baked into tortes, and tucked into crusts. They can fill spring rolls, taco shells, and soft tortillas. They can be crunchy or meltingly soft.

From twenty-five cuisines around the world, ranging from China to India, Mexico to Brazil, Egypt to Lebanon, and throughout the United States, these recipes have as their commonality savory flavors and a gustatory memory. You remember the dishes, and want to eat some of them again and again.

Some of the dishes are startlingly simple. Lois Freedman, the president of Jean-Georges Management and formerly a cook working with Jean-Georges Vongerichten at the four-star Lafayette, makes a corn pudding that is no more than grating fresh corn into a cast-iron pan, putting it in the oven, and after it thickens and forms a pale golden crust, taking it out of the oven and seasoning it with a little salt, pepper, butter, and a squeeze of lime juice. That's it. It is incredibly sweet and fresh.

Eli Zabar, the restaurateur, shares his egg salad recipe, and it, too, has a purity of flavor. He discovered in 1975 that if he halved the amount of egg whites, he could make an egg salad that was rich,

creamy, and, he said, "In the good sense of the word, eggy."

Daniel Humm, the executive chef of the four-star Eleven Madison Park, offers grilled circles of watermelon topped by cylinders of red, green, yellow, and orange tomatoes and drizzled with aged, thick, sweet balsamic vinegar.

Other recipes are more complex, like the braised cabbage balls from Didier Elena, the executive chef of Adour Alain Ducasse. The slivered cabbage has to be simmered. Leaves for wrapping have to be blanched. Then the balls are rolled and popped into the oven. The upside of the dish? The braising can be done the day before. The rolling and final cooking can be done the day of, and the presentation is beautiful: Each person gets two little balls, one red, one green, flavored by juniper berries, fleur de sel, pepper, lime zest, and a scant bit of broth. They are tender and aromatic.

Some of these dishes are vegan. Ayinde Howell, a thirty-four-year-old cook who was born to vegan restaurateurs in Tacoma, Washington, proves that through the alchemy of heat, tofu can be fried to look like browned bits of meat, which becomes the filling of a terrific enchilada, enlivened by onions, garlic, cumin, chile, sweet red bell peppers, and tomatoes.

Many of the recipes were inspired by the chef's mother's or grandmother's home cooking. One of John Fraser's favorite dishes is a homey Greek dish of green beans braised with tomatoes. He eats it at home, but won't serve it at his restaurant, Dovetail.

"It's ugly," he explained when I asked him why. Braised green beans are not bright, sparkling green. They turn dull and lose their vividness, shading into a dark olive. But what they lose in luster, they gain in flavor.

Many of the dishes are seasonal. All of them, however, are relatively inexpensive. And some—especially cabbage and potatoes—are the food that often fed the poor, whether in China or in Africa. But the food of the poor does not necessarily taste poor.

Marcus Samuelsson's Ethiopian dish of warmed cabbage and beans in spiced butter is so tasty, so subtly and brilliantly spiced, that after I first ate it with him and his wife, Maya, for breakfast, I ate it the next day with rice, again for breakfast. Then on the following day, I ate it yet again.

In the year and a half of writing this book, I became much more of a temporary vegetarian than I had been. Previously, I, like many of us, probably called myself a temporary vegetarian on the days I ate only a salad for lunch or a plate of pesto for dinner. At the same time, I was primarily a happy carnivore who ate meat once a day, if only a ham and cheese croissant. Now I'm a very satisfied temporary vegetarian who can skip meat for an entire day and often part of the following day.

By the end of the second day, however, I may want to eat a bowl of wonton or a half dozen steamed juicy buns, filled with minced pork. But I no longer crave a steak, rarely even a hamburger. I can get by on about two ounces of meat a day. As I was testing the recipes, I gave vegetarian dinner parties and loved them.

Why have I become much more of a temporary vegetarian?

Because I discovered as I cooked and ate my way through these recipes, I could be replete on a vegetarian diet, with all my taste buds and even the urge to chomp—to bite into something firm—deeply satisfied.

The ninety people who contributed recipes are not vegetarians, except for the aforementioned vegan chef. But all of the cooks understand robust flavors and the need for many textures—in other words, something crunchy or chewy. When a vegetarian dish lacks something crisp, these cooks add it. It takes the form of chopped nuts; raw, julienned vegetables; or a sprinkle of toasted black mustard seeds or toasted sesame seeds. There are croutons made of tofu for one dish, and a lacy cracker made of melted Argentine Reggianito cheese for another.

Of the chefs who contributed recipes, most of them said that ten years ago, perhaps 1 percent of their customers were vegetarian. Now, they suspect that about 5 to 7 percent are vegetarian. To make the vegetarians happy, the chefs offer a vegetarian entrée or at least make vegetarian appetizers and side dishes so tasty that you can build a meal from them. Steamed green beans and steamed asparagus are the side dishes of the past.

The recipes in this book are zesty and satisfying.

These recipes fill us up, much like meat, especially when served with rice or bread. I am Chinese, so Ma Po Tofu over rice is a perfect breakfast. It is silky, spicy, and has tiny bits of preserved Sichuan vegetable for crunch.

I read Michael Pollan's book *The Omnivore's Dilemma*. It is a chilling book when it focuses on industrially raised animals. Pigs have their tails chopped off, so each, in its confined space, won't gnaw the tail off the pig in front of it. Cows wallow around lagoons of manure. Such horrors have changed my mind, and the minds of many others, about how we want to cook and eat.

Now, when I am looking for the occasional chicken to roast for Thanksgiving, or for a sausage, I want the meat to come from a happy, free-ranging chicken or pig. However, finding that animal requires some serious shopping. And although there is excellent meat to be had at the Union Square Greenmarket, I am most enchanted by the vegetables, the fruit, and the flowers.

I live two blocks from the Greenmarket, and shop there at least once, if not twice, a week. I am seduced by the vegetables, and during the summer, when tomatoes are at their most fulsome, I keep a bowl of tomatoes on the kitchen counter with such boring regularity that a friend of my daughter's once asked in early October, "Are those the same five tomatoes your mother has kept since August?"

I search for peaches, guided by tips from people like Nick Fox, the deputy editor of the Dining Section at the *New York Times*. "Peaches?" he said one Saturday morning at the Greenmarket when we bumped into each other. "Go over to Ted Blew's on the north side. Look for the peaches with the bees buzzing around." Those peaches were the sweetest. The bees knew.

Eating vegetarian dishes is a newer delight for me, and an older one for many others.

From A to Z, then, the vegetables.

Asparagus signifies spring to most chefs, and the two recipes that feature it call for the large, fat fleshy variety. The vignarola, asparagus and artichokes in white wine, is a delicate dish, a sampling of the season's first vegetables. The bubbling asparagus gratin topped with a salad of endive and radicchio combines hot with cold, richness with tartness.

B includes beans, green ones and white ones, fresh ones and dried ones. There are braised green beans from both India and Greece. Julie Sahni starts with a sauté of onions, garlic, cumin, coriander, paprika, and chile flakes, then adds the beans and coconut milk. John Fraser makes his Greek beans. The beans in both dishes turn out dully colored and vividly flavored. Looks aren't everything.

In Europe, white beans, cooked until they are almost creamy, partner merrily with bitter greens. Gabriel Kreuther makes a soup of cranberry beans and kale that he ate growing up in Alsace. Jonnatan Leiva is Portuguese on his mother's side, and he makes a stew of white beans and radicchio.

Anita Lo creates a broccoli panzanella, where she roasts the broccoli first to bring out its sweetness, and then adds a walnut sauce and plump croutons. Jonathan Benno introduces one of his current, favorite vegetables: Broccoli Spigarello, a peppery yet just faintly sweet broccoli sold at the Greenmarket. For Tien Ho's hearty, zesty three-bean salad, he tops it with big, golden crisp croutons made from deep-fried tofu, in a moment of clever fusion cooking.

C is partly for cabbage and cauliflower, homely vegetables that some chefs believe are underused because they are considered poor people's food. That neglect is being amended in this book. Kurt Gutenbrunner makes a red cabbage salad in five minutes, enlivens it with walnut oil and lingonberry preserves, and suggests how to make it a complete meal: Add a sour brown bread like rye, and a cheese such as a Cheddar or a soft blue.

When cooked, cabbage can become very sweet and tender. Marcus Samuelsson and Didier Elena both use napa cabbage for their two dishes, because of its tenderness. Cabbage shows up in a multitude of cuisines, from Korea's kimchi pancakes to Floyd Cardoz's Indian Braised Cabbage to Hungary's cabbage strudel.

Michael Anthony's roasted Cauliflower with Almonds, Capers, and Raisins is one part of his arsenal of culinary tools that he used to court his wife, who, prior to this dish, did not like cauliflower. The cauliflower is cut thick, so that it is toothsome. Sprinkled with sliced almonds, capers, and raisins, it has crispy, sour, and sweet elements. It is finished off with a topping of toasted bread crumbs. In cooking vegetarian dishes, chefs learn that to add texture to vegetables, toasted bread crumbs and toasted nuts are excellent garnishes. Adam Weisell makes *Cauliflower Sformato*, a time-consuming, savory, delicate cauliflower flan. Although it takes two hours to make, it keeps in the refrigerator for three days.

Swiss chard, made into an Italian torta, and studded with raisins, olives, and cherry tomatoes, is a rich, festive dish that makes a great centerpiece. On the other hand, Heather Carlucci-Rodriguez's *Chana Punjabi*, Indian chickpea stew, is comfort food. It is gently spicy, and, when served over rice, a soothing, complete meal. So, too, Thai Green Curry Vegetables, made with eggplant, red bell pepper, zucchini, sweet potatoes, and green beans, in the familiar sauce of green curry paste and coconut milk, is a panoply of vegetables, each distinct, but bound by a winning sauce.

The joy of fresh, sweet corn is celebrated in a light, American corn chowder, in an Indonesian dish of corn fritters, and in Lois Freedman's delicious Corn Pudding, a recipe she created in 1994.

E is for eggs and endive. Eli Zabar's minimalist and rich Egg Salad Sandwich is here, as is John Fraser's Greek Egg Lemon Soup, bolstered by orzo. There is a Chinese version of steamed eggs, a dish that the Japanese also do with great finesse. The secret: Add cool broth to the beaten eggs and allow the froth of the beaten eggs to subside before steaming them, so that the surface is glassy smooth.

Endive can be eaten raw in a salad, or cooked until caramelized and yielding. Roland Caracostea makes a rich and beautiful Endive Cheese Tart inspired by a French woman he met on a train. Jordan Frosolone looked to Italy for his Braised Endives with Blood Oranges, Sicilian Pistachios, and Ricotta Salata.

G has a single, summery entry, a white grape gazpacho that Anthony Sasso brought back from Palafolls, in Catalonia, Spain.

H stands for the herbs that Persians love. In Iran, the people often have a platter of fresh herbs—mint, basil, dill, parsley—at the table to accompany the other dishes. In this dish, the greens—parsley, cilantro, scallions, lettuce—go into the frittata, and are mixed with ruby red barberries and crunchy chopped walnuts.

L includes leeks as a topping for a Provençal tart, and lentils in a savory, soothing soup from Kalustyan's, the famous spice shop in Manhattan's Little India.

M zeroes in on the mushroom, the vegetarian's faux meat. When chefs work with mushrooms, they almost always choose a trio of them, for the variety of flavors and textures. From China, they are braised until glistening and savory, and served on top of baby bok choy. Lettuce wraps are also stuffed with minced mushrooms, celery, carrots, scallions, tofu, and toasted pine nuts. Mushrooms and daikon make a delicate soup, while mushrooms and leeks make a comforting pot pie. Jean-Georges Vongerichten shares his Fragrant Mushroom Spring Rolls, Wrapped in Lettuce Cups, a recipe inspired by a food hawker in Singapore. There are also Mexican Mushroom Quesadillas and Roasted Mushrooms with Goat Cheese and Grits.

N is the catchall section for noodle and pasta dishes, whose origins are worldwide: Italy, China, America, Korea, Thailand, Malaysia, Vietnam. Most of the noodle dishes are served hot, like Mushroom and Chive Panfried Noodles, Pad Thai, or Orzotto with Zucchini and Pesto. Some, however, are served cold, like noodles with peanut sauce, and Michael Huynh's Vietnamese Noodle Salad.

O reveals the secret ingredient of John Schenk's vegetarian French onion soup. Instead of using beef stock, he adds miso.

P opens with a winsome miniature Brazilian tartlet filled with hearts of palm, segues to a sweet pea crostini, and on to roasted pepper tacos. But it is mostly devoted to the ever adaptable, mutable potato. The potato lends itself to a hotcake topped with a salad, or thinly sliced and mixed with Swiss chard for a rich, hearty gratin. From Lebanon comes *Batata Harra*, spicy, twice-fried potato cubes, which are then drizzled with a perky green sauce of cilantro, parsley, garlic, olive oil, and Aleppo pepper. Spain has the famous, ubiquitous tortilla, which is thinly sliced potato poached in a king's ransom of olive oil, drained, and then mixed with beaten eggs and cooked again in olive oil. It is served pale gold, and with each bite, you taste the subtle, fruity flavor of the olive oil. The Spanish eat it hot and straight out of the refrigerator, ice cold with a dollop of mayonnaise, with equal joy.

R is devoted to rice, including an austere but appealing Japanese fifteen-grain rice pot topped with mushrooms, julienned carrots, edamame, and toasted sesame seeds. Korea is the home of *Bibimbap*, the rice casserole topped with zucchini, mushrooms, bean sprouts, spinach, radish, and carrot. What gives *bibimbap* its wonderful mix of textures and flavors is that each vegetable is blanched or sautéed and seasoned separately. From India comes the classic Lemon Rice with an extravagant toss of roasted peanuts. The *Arroz de Verduras,* or Vegetable Rice, from Portugal, is rice cooked in a sofrito—garlic, onions, sweet paprika, tomato, and saffron. Then George Mendes adds corn, edamame, peas, and olives, and bakes it until the top is golden and the bottom is crusty.

S leads to another Persian or Iranian dish, soybeans cooked with garlic and dill. In Tehran, Maryam Zomorodi made it with fresh fava beans. Since I am allergic to the work involved with favas, I substituted edamame instead. I tried frozen favas; they turned into mush. However, the edamame works. The Indian classic, spinach saag, becomes even tastier when topped with fried potato balls.

T is partly for tofu, which in Tyler Kord's hands is not boring. In his General Tso's Tofu Sub, the tofu is dipped in panko, fried until golden, and layered with edamame puree, pickled cucumbers, and a piquant sauce. Susur Lee makes a perfect rendition of the classic Ma Po Tofu, silken tofu made spicy.

Tomatoes are shown off in many forms. There is a Moroccan stuffed tomato, filled with zucchini, cilantro, and pistachios. A Mediterranean-inspired tartine has roasted tomatoes, grilled eggplant, melted goat cheese, and olive tapenade on crusty, coarse toast.

V. is for a mélange of vegetables in a saffron broth.

W includes Daniel Humm's simple grilled watermelon topped by four batons of heirloom tomatoes, preferably one red, one orange, one yellow, and one green.

Z celebrates the zucchini, whether it's in Louise Beylerian's Zucchini and Cheese Pie, a dish she first ate in Cairo, where she grew up, or in Julian Medina's Zucchini and Squash Tacos, or in Aytekin Yar's Turkish Zucchini Pancakes.

A

Asparagus and Artichokes in White Wine (Vignarola)

Adapted from Matteo Bergamini, Executive Chef, SD26

TIME: *35 minutes*
YIELD: *2 servings*

½ cup extra-virgin olive oil

½ cup dry white wine, plus 1 to
2 tablespoons Chenin Blanc
or Sauvignon Blanc
(optional)

½ cup finely chopped onion

4 baby artichokes, outer green
leaves discarded and stems
trimmed, cut lengthwise into
quarters or sixths

7 large asparagus, peeled,
ends trimmed, cut diagonally
into ½-inch slices

¼ cup fresh or frozen
English peas

3 scallions, trimmed and
discarded, cut diagonally
into ½-inch slices

Salt and freshly ground
black pepper

Large, thin shavings of
Pecorino Romano,
for garnish

At Tony May's restaurant, SD26, which is the Madison Square Park in-carnation of his previous place, San Domenico on Central Park South, the menu lists a dish called Vignarola. It's a sprightly, fresh seasonal mix of fava beans, baby artichokes, asparagus, and peas in a light, white wine sauce. Paper-thin shavings of Pecorino Romano garnish the top, resting lightly on the vegetables.

To Tony May and Matteo Bergamini, the executive chef, an essential ingredient is the seasonal fava bean, which needs to be first shelled, then peeled. The adaptation here is intended for the home cook, and avoids the troublesome—though tasty—fava bean.

1. In a medium saucepan, combine the olive oil and ½ cup white wine. Place over medium-low heat and bring to a simmer. Add the onion and artichokes, and simmer gently for 5 minutes. Add the asparagus, and simmer for 3 to 4 minutes.

2. Add the peas, and simmer for 2 more minutes. Add the scallions, and simmer for 1 more minute. Season with salt and pepper to taste. The sauce should be the consistency of heavy cream; if necessary, add 1 or 2 tablespoons of wine and cook for 2 minutes more.

3. Divide the vegetables in the oil and wine sauce between two serving bowls. Garnish with shavings of Pecorino Romano and a twist of black pepper.

Kenmare's Asparagus Gratin

Adapted from Joey Campanaro, Executive Chef, Kenmare

TIME: *1 hour and 10 minutes*
YIELD: *4 servings*

1 cup heavy cream

2 shallots, finely chopped

1/4 cup dry white wine,
    such as Chenin Blanc or
    Sauvignon Blanc

1/4 cup pecans

1/4 cup panko bread crumbs

1 bunch fresh spring
    asparagus, peeled and cut
    diagonally into 1/2-inch slices,
    ends discarded

1/4 cup grated fontina
    cheese

1/4 cup grated Parmigiano-
    Reggiano cheese

2 large endives, trimmed,
    and cut into diagonal
    1-inch-wide slices

1/2 small head of radicchio,
    trimmed, and leaves torn
    into 1-inch pieces

Extra-virgin olive oil,
    as needed

"Every March, I think about asparagus," said Joey Campanaro, the executive chef of Kenmare in SoHo, who loves the vegetable for its versatility. "I make purees with it, I tempura it, I grill it."

At Kenmare, he introduced asparagus gratin—sliced, peeled asparagus baked until golden and bubbly in a sauce of cream, white wine, and cheese.

Once the asparagus comes out of the oven, he sprinkles it with a mix of toasted panko and toasted ground pecans, and then, in a brilliant flourish, he tops it with a salad—a toss of endive and radicchio lightly dressed with olive oil, lemon juice, salt, and pepper.

The dish is cold upon hot. Red and green leaves first flutter above the tender asparagus, which poke up through the sauce. Once the radicchio and endive settle into the sauce and get hot, "they become more tender, and the bitterness, especially in the radicchio, is alleviated," Mr. Campanaro said. The dish is as pretty as it is tasty.

1. Preheat the oven to 350°F. In a medium saucepan, combine the cream, shallots, and wine. Place over medium heat and simmer until reduced by half, 20 to 30 minutes.

2. Spread the pecans on a baking sheet and bake, stirring once or twice, until toasted, 10 to 15 minutes. Meanwhile, place a skillet over low heat, add the panko, and stir until golden brown, about 5 minutes. Remove from the heat and set aside to cool. When the pecans are toasted, remove from the oven and set aside to cool.

Fresh lemon juice, as needed
Salt and freshly ground
    black pepper

3. Increase the oven temperature to 400°F. When the pecans are cool, place in a blender and chop for a few seconds until coarsely ground. Mix with the panko and set aside.

4. In a mixing bowl, combine the asparagus, reduced cream, fontina, and Parmigiano-Reggiano. Mix well and place in a gratin dish about 10 inches long and 4 inches wide, or another shallow ovenproof baking dish. Bake until the asparagus is tender, the sauce is bubbling and the top is turning golden, 6 to 10 minutes. Remove from the oven and top with the pecan–bread crumb mixture. In a separate bowl, mix the endives and radicchio with olive oil, lemon juice, and salt and pepper to taste. Spread over the top of the asparagus gratin. Serve hot.

B

Bean Confit (Vegan)

Adapted from Bill Telepan, Executive Chef, Telepan

TIME: 2 hours,
plus overnight soaking
YIELD: 2 to 3 servings

½ cup dried cranberry beans,
Italian white beans, or other
white beans, soaked
overnight in cold water
1 sprig oregano
1 sprig rosemary
2 garlic cloves, peeled
1½ cups extra-virgin olive oil
Salt

Bill Telepan, the executive chef of Telepan in Manhattan, loves bean confit, which is cooked beans that are then baked in olive oil and scented with oregano, rosemary, and garlic. He likes not just the flavor, but also the adaptability of the beans. "I'll crush the beans and spread it on toast, and serve it with cherry tomatoes, cut in half, and splashed with olive oil, red wine vinegar, and balsamic vinegar," he said. "I love the sweetness of the balsamic, and the red wine vinegar gives it acidity."

The beans can also be mixed with brown rice, served warm, and drizzled with lemon juice. Or they can be mixed with farro. When the beans are finished, he suggests using the flavored oil for a vinaigrette.

Mr. Telepan has a few simple rules on cooking beans:

Rule #1. Do not let the pot boil, because the turbulence will cause the bean skins to separate from the beans and float off, and you'll get unevenly cooked beans.

Rule #2. You cannot salt the beans when they are cooking because they will never get soft.

Rule #3. Resist the urge to stir. Stirring breaks the beans into pieces.

1. In a heavy ovenproof, flameproof pot, combine the beans and 4 cups cold water. Place over high heat to bring to a boil, then reduce the heat to low. Simmer gently, uncovered, until moderately tender, 30 to 45 minutes; do not boil or stir. As the beans cook, check periodically to be sure they remain covered with water, adding hot water as necessary.

{continued}

2. Preheat the oven to 300°F. Drain the beans, then return them to the pot and add the oregano, rosemary, and garlic. Cover with the oil. Transfer to the oven and cook, uncovered, until the beans are completely tender, 30 to 45 minutes. Remove from the heat and season to taste with salt. For best flavor, allow to cool to room temperature, then cover and refrigerate overnight or up to 7 days.

3. To serve, gently reheat the beans and serve with a slotted spoon, leaving the oil in the pot. Serve warm on top of a salad, or crushed, sprinkled with a few drops of olive oil and spread on top of toast. May also be served mixed with cooked rice or farro.

Bihari Green Beans Masala (Vegan)

Adapted from Julie Sahni, Cookbook Author and Teacher

TIME: 40 minutes
YIELD: 2 to 3 servings

2 tablespoons vegetable oil
  or light olive oil
2 tablespoons sliced almonds
½ cup finely chopped onion
3 large garlic cloves,
  finely chopped
1 teaspoon ground cumin
1 teaspoon ground coriander
1 teaspoon sweet paprika
½ teaspoon red chile
  pepper flakes
¾ teaspoon kosher salt
¾ cup coconut milk
¾ pound green beans,
  trimmed and cut into
  1-inch pieces
1 teaspoon lime juice
2 tablespoons chopped
  cilantro
Plain cooked rice or roti
  flatbread, for serving
  (optional)

This succulent green bean dish, in a gently spiced sauce of coconut milk, is from Bihar, a state in India. "It is an everyday, simple dish that is several hundred years old," said Julie Sahni, a cooking teacher and author of eight cookbooks, including *Classic Indian Cooking* (William Morrow, 1980), which is in its thirty-eighth printing.

She prepared the dish in her home in Brooklyn, where she gives cooking classes. On her shelf, she had unmarked glass jars for her spices, arranged by color. How does one tell one white ingredient from another, or a red-orange one from a burnt orange one?

You don't, unless you're Ms. Sahni or a kindred professional. The ignorant have to turn the jar upside down and read the label on the bottom. "This is to test the students," she said, smiling.

The dish requires fresh green string beans, not French haricot verts or Asian long beans, which are thinner and more dense. "The string beans will plump up and absorb some of the sauce," said Ms. Sahni.

When she added the beans to the bubbling ochre sauce, she covered the sauté pan to help the spices penetrate. When the beans were nearly ready she took a handful of fresh cilantro and chopped it, stems and all, which is an Indian tradition. She finished the beans with a squeeze of fresh lime juice, the cilantro, and for crunch and contrast, toasted slivered almonds. Rice is the natural accompaniment.

The recipe can be adapted for 12 ounces of raw cauliflower, carrots, eggplant, or brussels sprouts. For the eggplant, she uses the long, slender Japanese ones and cuts them on the diagonal, in 1-inch slices.

{*continued*}

She trims and peels the carrots, and cuts them like the eggplant, in 1-inch diagonal slices. For the cauliflower, she uses the florets, and cuts them in pieces that are $1^{1}/_{2}$ inches in diameter. For brussels sprouts, she trims and discards the stems, and cuts the vegetable in half. Very fresh cauliflower cooks in 4 minutes, the other vegetables in 6 minutes, Ms. Sahni said.

1. Heat the oil in a 3-quart sauté pan over medium heat. Add the almonds and cook, stirring, until light golden. Remove from the heat and transfer the almonds to a plate or bowl; set aside for garnish.

2. Add the onion, garlic, cumin, coriander, paprika, chile pepper flakes, and salt to the unwashed sauté pan, and return to medium heat. Sauté until the onion is tender and begins to fry, about 4 minutes.

3. Add the coconut milk and green beans. Mix well and bring to a boil. Reduce the heat to medium-low and cook, covered, until the beans are tender, about 6 minutes.

4. Sprinkle the beans with the lime juice and toss lightly. Transfer to a warmed serving dish and garnish with the almonds and cilantro. If desired, serve accompanied by plain cooked rice or roti flatbread.

Cranberry Bean and Kale Soup (Vegan)

Adapted from Gabriel Kreuther, Executive Chef, The Modern

TIME: 1 hour and 10 minutes
YIELD: 4 to 6 servings

FOR THE BEANS:

½ pound fresh shelled
   cranberry beans (from about
   1½ pounds in the pod),
   or ½ pound dried cranberry
   beans, soaked overnight in
   cold water and drained
1 medium tomato
1 small onion, cut into 8 pieces
2 sprigs thyme
1 bay leaf
1 sprig rosemary
1 small carrot, peeled and
   halved lengthwise
4 whole garlic cloves, peeled

FOR THE SOUP:

Salt
1 pound kale, center stems
   removed and discarded
1 pound cherry tomatoes

At The Modern restaurant at the Museum of Modern Art, Gabriel Kreuther, the executive chef, makes a cranberry bean and kale soup, dotted with crushed cherry tomatoes, that was inspired by a rustic soup he had as a child growing up on a farm in Niederschaeffolsheim, in the Alsace region of France.

"When it was winter, into April, once a week we made a bean soup, with beans, carrots, celeriacs," he said. For greens, his family tossed in kale, or borage or cabbage. "You can also use collard greens, or if salad greens grow too big, you can use them, too," he said. "Nothing is lost."

Mr. Kreuther has refined the soup, and has made it into a hearty, visually striking dish. The kale is cut into fine, slender strands. The broth, which is more thin than thick, has a fresh, light taste because it is made solely from the cooking liquids of the beans and kale.

By plunging the cooked kale into an ice bath, Mr. Kreuther preserves its emerald green color. The finished soup is distinctly tricolor: The beans are creamy beige, the tomatoes bright red, and the kale brilliant green.

1. For the beans: Rinse the beans under cold water. Place in a stockpot and cover with 2½ quarts cold water. On a large piece of cheesecloth, place the whole tomato, onion pieces, thyme, bay leaf, rosemary, carrot, and garlic, and tie together to loosely contain the contents. Add to the pot and press to submerge. Bring to a boil, then simmer until the beans are tender, about 45 minutes.

{continued}

2 tablespoons extra-virgin
   olive oil
1 large onion, finely chopped
6 garlic cloves, thinly sliced
Freshly ground black pepper
Extra-virgin olive oil,
   for drizzling
1½ teaspoons minced
   marjoram leaves, for garnish
1½ teaspoons minced parsley
   leaves, for garnish

2. For the soup: While the beans cook, fill another large pot with 4 quarts water, add 1 tablespoon salt, and bring to a boil. Set aside a bowl of ice water. Add the kale leaves to the boiling water, blanch for 5 minutes, then use tongs or a slotted spoon to transfer to the ice water; reserve the cooking water. When the leaves are completely chilled, drain well, squeezing out the excess water. Chop finely into slender strips and set aside.

3. Return the kale cooking water to a boil. Set aside a bowl of ice water. Prick each cherry tomato with a fork, blanch in boiling water for 5 seconds, then drain and place in ice water until chilled. Peel the tomatoes and set aside. Reserve the cooking liquid.

4. In a large skillet over medium heat, combine the olive oil, onion, garlic, and a pinch of salt. Sauté until the onion is tender, about 5 minutes. Add the cherry tomatoes and sauté until the tomatoes soften and begin to break up, about 5 minutes. Using a potato masher, gently crush the tomatoes without destroying their shape.

5. Drain the cooked beans, reserving the cooking liquid. Discard the cheesecloth and its contents. Return half the beans to the pot, and mash with a potato masher until they are fairly smooth. Add the remaining beans, the contents of the skillet, 1 quart cooking liquid from the beans, and 1 quart cooking liquid from the kale. Return to high heat to bring to a boil, then reduce the heat and simmer for 10 minutes. Skim the surface, discarding the froth. Season to taste with salt and pepper, and add more cooking liquids, up to 1 quart, as desired; the broth should remain thin.

6. To serve, add the chopped kale and cook only until heated through, 30 to 60 seconds. Place in heated soup bowls, and garnish each bowl with a drizzle of olive oil and a sprinkling of marjoram and parsley.

Green Beans Braised in Tomato Sauce with Country Toast (Vegan)

Adapted from John Fraser, Chef-Owner, Dovetail

TIME: 45 minutes
YIELD: 2 servings

2 beefsteak tomatoes

2½ tablespoons plus
  1 teaspoon extra-virgin
  olive oil

1 garlic clove, thinly sliced

1 shallot, minced

½ pound green beans,
  trimmed

¼ teaspoon crushed chile
  flakes or Aleppo pepper

Salt and ground white pepper
  to taste

Two ½-inch-thick country
  bread slices

8 medium basil leaves,
  sliced into chiffonade

Green beans braised with tomatoes, shallot, and garlic and served over thick slices of crusty, country bread is one of the favorite dishes of John Fraser, the chef/owner of Dovetail in Manhattan, who is part Greek on his mother's side. It was a staple of his childhood.

John Fraser grew up in Yucaipa, California, and in the backyard, the family grew runner beans and green beans, and then braised either one of them with tomatoes. "You spread the beans over the bottom of the pan, because you want them to have their own space," he said. "You can eat it hot or cold."

As delicious as the dish is, he does not put it on his menu. Neither will he cook the beans and tomatoes on request.

"They're ugly," he said. "When you have a green bean and braise it, it doesn't look good. Things like this are best for home." The bread has to be thick and crusty, otherwise it will collapse under the saucy beans. The dish also has to be eaten quickly, or, as he said, "The bread will sog."

1. Bring a small saucepan of water to a boil. Add the tomatoes, and simmer until the skin begins to break, 1 to 2 minutes. Drain; rinse under cold water until cooled. Peel the tomatoes, cut in half, discard the seeds, and cut into small cubes. Place in a bowl and set aside.

2. In a medium saucepan over medium-low heat, heat 2½ tablespoons of the olive oil until shimmering. Add the garlic and stir until

{continued}

barely translucent; do not allow to brown. Add the shallot and stir until translucent. Add the tomatoes, raise the heat to medium, and stir constantly until the juices have evaporated, 5 to 7 minutes.

3. Add the green beans, spreading them evenly in the pan. Add the chile flakes and reduce the heat to medium-low. Simmer, covered, until the beans are fork tender, about 15 minutes. Season with salt and pepper to taste.

4. Brush the remaining 1 teaspoon olive oil on the bread slices, and toast until golden brown. Place a slice on each of two plates, and spoon an equal portion of green beans and tomatoes on each slice. Sprinkle with basil and serve immediately.

Green Bean Casserole

Adapted from Joaquin Baca, Chef-Owner, Brooklyn Star

TIME: *1 hour and 15 minutes*
YIELD: *8 servings*

1 pound button mushrooms,
  sliced
2 small red onions, chopped
4 ounces (1 stick)
  unsalted butter
2 garlic cloves, chopped
1 tablespoon fresh thyme
  leaves
1 cup heavy cream
1 cup vegetable stock
Salt and freshly ground
  black pepper
2 pounds green beans,
  trimmed
1/4 cup sliced toasted almonds
1/2 cup fine dry bread crumbs
1/2 cup vegetable oil
1/3 cup all-purpose flour
6 pearl onions, thinly sliced

Joaquin Baca has cooked Asian-flavored noodles with David Chang at the Momofuku restaurants and has lived in the Philippines, Bolivia, and Uruguay. But his roots are Texan, and he has never lost touch with American comfort food: barbecued ribs, corn bread, chicken-fried steak.

"It's what I like to eat," he said. "It's what I cook."

When he was a boy in the 1970s, his mother often prepared a classic 1950s American dish: a green bean casserole made moist with Campbell's cream of mushroom soup and crisp with fried onion rings, straight from another can. When he was a student at the University of Texas at Austin, he upgraded the dish by making it from scratch, including the mushroom soup and the fried onion rings. "I just made this up myself," he said. "There's no sense in buying a product you can make yourself."

When he opened the Brooklyn Star this year in Williamsburg, he decided to serve only the food he loves, including the green bean casserole. It arrives in a small cast-iron skillet, bubbling and sizzling, fresh from the huge brick oven. The beans are tender, the mushrooms are abundant, and the freshly toasted slivered almonds and the deep-fried pearl onions are crunchy. It is 1950s redux—but so much better.

1. In a food processor, combine half the mushrooms and both onions. Puree to form a paste and set aside. In a large, wide saucepan over medium heat, melt the butter and add the remaining mushrooms.

{continued}

Stir, increase the heat to high, and sauté until the mushrooms release their liquid, then become golden and begin to crisp around the edges.

2. Add the garlic and thyme, and stir for about 30 seconds. Add the mushroom-onion paste and reduce the heat to medium-low. Cook, stirring constantly, 10 to 15 minutes. Add the cream and stock, and season with salt and pepper to taste. At this point, the mushroom mixture may be cooled, covered, and refrigerated for up to 24 hours.

3. Bring a large pot of water to a boil and set aside a large bowl of ice water. Add the beans to the boiling water and cook until bright green and barely tender, about 1 minute. Drain and immediately plunge into ice water. Drain well.

4. In a large mixing bowl, combine the green beans, mushroom mixture, almonds, and ¼ cup bread crumbs. Transfer to a 9 by 12 by 2-inch baking dish, patting down to compact and level the mixture. Sprinkle with the remaining ¼ cup bread crumbs. Bake, uncovered, until the beans are tender and the top is lightly browned, about 35 minutes.

5. To garnish, place the oil in a small skillet and heat until it simmers. Place the flour in a mixing bowl and season lightly with salt and pepper. Add the sliced pearl onions, toss to coat, and fry until golden, 30 to 45 seconds. Drain on paper towels and sprinkle on the casserole.

Catalan-Style Radicchio and White Beans (Vegan)

Adapted from Jonnatan Leiva,
Executive Chef, 10 Downing Food & Wine

TIME: 1¹/₂ hours, plus overnight soaking of the beans
YIELD: 5 servings

FOR THE BEANS:

6 ounces (about 1 cup)
   dried cannellini beans
1 garlic clove
1 sprig thyme
1 to 2 vegetable bouillon cubes

FOR THE RADICCHIO:

3 tablespoons olive oil
1 head of radicchio, stem and
   core removed, leaves cut or
   torn into 1¹/₂-inch squares
¹/₈ teaspoon crushed red
   pepper flakes
Salt and freshly ground
   black pepper
1 garlic clove, minced
1 tablespoon minced
   fresh parsley
Cracked black pepper,
   for garnish

"I love beans and bitter greens," said Jonnatan Leiva, the executive chef at 10 Downing Food & Wine, who made a beautiful stew of ruby red radicchio and creamy white beans. "This dish is actually my heritage, which is Latino." His maternal grandparents were from the Catalan area of Spain, moved to El Salvador, and then to San Francisco, where he grew up.

"My grandmother picked up vegetables from the market, and she always brought back bitter greens," he said. He likes how the "rounded richness of the beans" pairs with the greens, or, in this case, the reds—the gloriously colored radicchio. Although most people would consider this a dish for winter, Mr. Leiva eats it year-round, even in spring and summer.

If radicchio is not available, Mr. Leiva suggests substituting escarole. The taste will be stunning, but you will miss the color of the radicchio.

1. For the beans: Place the beans in a bowl and add cold water to cover by 2 inches. Allow to soak overnight. The next day, drain, rinse with cold water, and drain again.

2. In a medium pot, combine the beans, garlic, thyme, and cold water to cover by 2 inches. Place over high heat to bring to a boil. Reduce the heat to medium, and simmer until tender, 25 to 45 minutes; do not salt the water. When the beans are tender, add 1 to 2 bouillon

{continued}

cubes to taste, and cook 5 minutes more; the liquid should be slightly salted. Drain the beans, reserving the liquid; discard the garlic and thyme. Set the beans and reserved liquid aside.

3. For the radicchio: In a large skillet over medium heat, heat 2 tablespoons of oil. Add the radicchio, turning to coat with the oil. Add the pepper flakes, and season with salt and pepper to taste. Cook, stirring occasionally, until tender, 7 to 10 minutes. Remove from the heat and set aside.

4. In a separate skillet over medium heat, add the remaining 1 tablespoon olive oil. Add the garlic and sauté until lightly browned, about 2 minutes. Add the beans and 2 cups of the reserved cooking liquid. Simmer until the liquid becomes somewhat creamy, 5 to 10 minutes. Add the radicchio and parsley, and simmer 10 minutes more, adding more of the reserved cooking liquid if the mixture seems too thick. Serve in bowls, garnished with a sprinkling of cracked black pepper.

Summer Three-Bean Salad with Tofu and Soy Vinaigrette (Vegan)

Adapted from Tien Ho, Executive Chef and Co-Owner, Má Pêche

TIME: *1 hour*
YIELD: *4 main-course or 6 appetizer servings*

FOR THE TOFU-SOY VINAIGRETTE:

1 cup silken tofu

½ cup soy sauce

2 tablespoons sugar

2 tablespoons sambal oelek chile paste

2 tablespoons sherry vinegar

1 tablespoon sesame oil

1 cup canola oil

FOR THE RADISHES AND BEANS:

1 pound radishes, preferably a mix of different kinds, trimmed and thinly sliced

Salt

2 pounds fresh beans, preferably a mix of 3 kinds, such as green, yellow wax, and Romano, or haricot verts, snow peas, and sugar snap peas, trimmed

"I was a vegetarian for a year, in 1994, when I was at the University of Texas at Austin," said Tien Ho, the executive chef and co-owner, with David Chang, of Má Pêche in Manhattan. "It was for all the wrong reasons."

Which were?

"A girl," he said.

Nevertheless, he pays homage to vegetables, and in the summer, he creates a three-bean salad with radishes to showcase the green beans, pale yellow wax beans, and Romano beans that are in season. "It could be haricots verts, regular green beans, sugar snaps," Mr. Ho said. "It's all about the dressing."

The sprightly, tangy dressing blends silken tofu with chile paste, canola oil, sherry vinegar, soy sauce, and a bit of sugar. "The salad is so meaty; it has so much protein; it has big flavors, and creaminess without fattiness," Mr. Ho said. "It's the silken tofu that gives it creaminess."

To garnish the salad, Mr. Ho makes tofu croutons. He deep-fries cubes of firm tofu that have been patted dry and dredged in cornstarch until they are crisp and golden. Finally, he sprinkles the salad with toasted sesame seeds.

Mr. Ho, who is Vietnamese, said he was inspired by Japanese cuisine, which has a tofu dressing, and by the fact that both the Chinese and the Japanese fry tofu until crisp outside. "Nothing is new," he said.

{continued}

FOR THE TOFU CROUTONS:

4 cups vegetable oil, or as
    needed

2 tablespoons cornstarch

½ pound firm tofu, patted dry
    and cut into ½-inch cubes

Salt

1 to 2 tablespoons black
    sesame seeds, lightly
    toasted

1 to 2 tablespoons white
    sesame seeds, lightly
    toasted

The dressing, which can be refrigerated for up to a week, works with any firm vegetable, like asparagus or broccoli, but it is not compatible with a baby lettuce salad because it would overwhelm the greens.

1. For the tofu-soy vinaigrette: In a blender, combine the tofu, soy sauce, sugar, sambal oelek, vinegar, and sesame oil. Blend until smooth. With the motor running at medium-low speed, slowly add the canola oil; the vinaigrette will become very thick. May be covered and refrigerated for up to a week.

2. For the radishes and beans: Prepare two bowls of ice mixed with water. Place the sliced radishes in one of the ice baths. Bring a large pot of heavily salted water to a boil. Add the beans and boil until they are crisp-tender, about 4 minutes. Drain under cold water, then place in the remaining ice bath to chill. Drain well and set aside.

3. For the tofu croutons: Pour the oil into a wok or small deep-fryer over high heat and heat to 350°F. Meanwhile, put the cornstarch into a wide, shallow bowl and add the tofu, tossing gently to coat. Working in batches, if needed, deep-fry the tofu until golden and crispy, 5 to 6 minutes. Using a slotted spoon, transfer to paper towels to drain. Season with salt and set aside.

4. Drain the radishes well and place in a large bowl. Add the blanched beans and toss to mix. Add the vinaigrette to taste, reserving any excess for another use. Mix well and season with salt to taste. To serve, place in individual serving plates or bowls, top with the tofu croutons, and sprinkle with black and white sesame seeds.

White Bean Soup (Vegan)

Adapted from Michael Psilakis, Executive Chef-Owner, Kefi

TIME: 1¹/₂ hours, plus overnight
   soaking of the beans
YIELD: 6 servings

¹/₄ cup plus 4 tablespoons
   extra-virgin olive oil
1 medium onion, cut into
   small dice
2 carrots, cut into small dice
3 celery stalks, cut into
   small dice
1¹/₂ cups dried cannellini
   beans, soaked overnight
2 bay leaves
Salt and freshly ground
   black pepper
¹/₂ cup fresh bread crumbs
3 scallions, trimmed
   and chopped
1 tomato, cut into small dice
6 tablespoons lemon juice
4 ounces baby spinach leaves
¹/₄ cup chopped fresh parsley
   leaves
¹/₄ cup chopped fresh dill

Michael Psilakis understands the beauty of fresh lemon juice.

"If you want to bring spring into winter, add herbs and acidity," said Mr. Psilakis, the executive chef and a partner in Kefi in Manhattan.

He was making a soulful white bean soup, and toward the end of the preparation, he deglazed scallions and diced tomatoes with lemon juice. At the very end, he tossed in a handful of minced parsley and dill. "The lemon juice and herbs brighten the dish," he said. "Acid is not an ingredient. It's a seasoning, like salt and pepper."

Mr. Psilakis grew up in East Northport on Long Island, where his mother, Georgia, taught him the basis of the soup.

"You can take this soup anywhere you want," he said. "The consistency is what you want it to be; some people want it thick, some people want it thin. You can add chile flakes or jalapeño, while you're sautéing the scallions and tomatoes. You can garnish it with toasted bread crumbs and dried lemon zest."

He never tires of it, even though he has made it for more than twenty years.

1. In a large pot over medium-high heat, heat ¹/₄ cup olive oil until shimmering. Add the onion, carrots, and celery, and sauté until the onions are translucent and the carrots are crisp-tender, 5 to 8 minutes.

{continued}

Add 3 1/2 quarts of water, the beans, and the bay leaves. Season lightly with salt and pepper to taste. Simmer until the beans are tender, about 45 minutes.

2. While the beans are simmering, make the bread crumb garnish. Place a small skillet over a low flame, add 2 tablespoons of the olive oil and the bread crumbs, and stir until golden brown. Transfer to a plate to cool; set aside.

3. When the beans are tender, pour one-third into a blender and allow to cool until no longer steaming. Puree and mix back into the pot of soup.

4. In a skillet over medium-high heat, heat the remaining 2 tablespoons olive oil until shimmering. Add the scallions and sauté for 1 minute. Add the tomato and sauté for 2 minutes. Add the lemon juice and stir until evaporated, 2 to 3 minutes. Add to the pot of beans. Add the spinach and simmer until wilted, about 3 minutes. Add the parsley and dill, and adjust the salt to taste. To serve, ladle into bowls and garnish with bread crumbs.

Broccoli Panzanella with Walnut Sauce and Basil (Vegan)

Adapted from Anita Lo, Executive Chef-Owner, Annisa

TIME: 45 minutes
YIELD: 3 to 4 servings

FOR THE BROCCOLI:

12 ounces broccoli, florets cut
   into pieces 1 inch long and
   stem peeled and cut into
   pieces 1 inch long and
   ½ inch thick
3 tablespoons olive oil
1 large garlic clove, minced
Pinch of red pepper flakes
Salt and freshly ground
   black pepper

FOR THE WALNUT SAUCE:

½ cup walnut pieces, toasted
1 large garlic clove, minced
3 tablespoons extra-virgin
   olive oil
Pinch of finely grated
   lemon zest
Salt and freshly ground
   black pepper

To Anita Lo, the executive chef and owner of Annisa in Manhattan, the Italian panzanella, a bread salad often tossed with tomatoes, capers, onions, and olives, is "a summery dish and a good use of day-old bread."

She has reinvented the panzanella for fall and winter by bypassing the tomatoes and making it with roasted broccoli that is crisp-tender and emerald green. "By roasting the broccoli, it makes it taste a little more cold weather–like," she said. "I love how roasting brings out the sweetness of the broccoli."

She tosses the toasted bread cubes with olive oil and lemon, and adds a sauce made of toasted walnuts, garlic, olive oil, and lemon zest. "Walnuts have protein and crunch, and you get an added richness," she said.

1. For the broccoli: Preheat the oven to 425°F. In a mixing bowl, combine the broccoli, olive oil, garlic, and red pepper flakes. Season with salt and pepper to taste. Spread across a baking sheet or shallow roasting pan, and roast until the broccoli is crisp-tender and is beginning to brown, 15 to 20 minutes. Meanwhile, prepare the walnut sauce.

2. For the walnut sauce: In a dry skillet or toaster oven, toast the walnut pieces until fragrant and lightly browned. Place in a blender with the garlic, olive oil, and lemon zest. Blend until smooth, adding just enough water to make a thick yet pourable sauce. Season with salt and pepper to taste.

{continued}

FOR ASSEMBLY:

1 day-old baguette, crust
  discarded and remaining
  cut into ³/₄- to 1-inch dice
1 tablespoon lemon juice,
  or to taste
¹/₄ cup extra-virgin olive oil,
  for drizzling
Salt and freshly ground
  black pepper
¹/₄ cup julienned basil leaves
Parmigiano-Reggiano shavings
  (optional)

3. For assembly: Spread the diced bread on a baking sheet and bake until crisp and golden, 5 to 10 minutes. Transfer to a bowl and add the lemon juice, olive oil, and salt and pepper to taste. Add the broccoli (there should be equal parts broccoli to bread) and mix lightly.

4. On a serving platter or in a shallow bowl, spread the walnut sauce and pile the broccoli and panzanella on top. Garnish with the julienned basil and, if desired, shaved Parmigiano-Reggiano.

Broccoli Spigarello (Vegan)

Adapted from Jonathan Benno, Chef, Lincoln Ristorante

TIME: *15 minutes*
YIELD: *2 to 3 servings*

Salt

3 cups broccoli spigarello
leaves or broccoli rabe
leaves (stems discarded)

3 tablespoons extra-virgin
olive oil

2 1/2 teaspoons minced garlic

Pinch of chile flakes

Gnocchi or risotto, for serving
(optional)

At Lincoln Ristorante, the $20 million, 150-seat restaurant at Lincoln Center that was many years in the planning, Jonathan Benno, the chef, said he would be happy to demonstrate one simple, tasty side dish.

It was broccoli spigarello, a broccoli native to Italy. Mr. Benno buys the broccoli, crates at a time, from Rick Bishop of Mountain Sweet Berry Farm in Roscoe, New York, who brings the broccoli spigarello to the Union Square Greenmarket on Wednesdays and Saturdays. Mr. Bishop sells it for $3 a bunch, which, stems discarded, makes 1 1/2 cups of leaves, or one good-sized serving. Leaves come large or small. Mr. Benno chooses the smaller, more tender ones.

"The star of the show is the broccoli," Mr. Benno said. "It's between a broccoli and a rapini. It has a slightly peppery flavor, like a broccoli rabe."

What it also has is moments of an underlying sweetness, especially at the end of the season, which is mid-November. "The cold weather brings out the sweetness," said Mr. Bishop, who grows 4,000 pounds a year, from May through mid-November.

Mr. Benno's preparation of the broccoli, which he offers as a small plate when in season, is simple. He blanches it until tender in heavily salted water. "It should taste like the sea," he said. "No—the Dead Sea." He plunges it into an ice bath to stop the cooking and retain the brilliant emerald green color. Then he sweats garlic in olive oil, adds the broccoli and a pinch of chile flakes, and voilà.

{continued}

With the broccoli, he served tender, melt-in-your-mouth potato gnocchi.

The combination worked.

1. Prepare a large bowl of ice water and set aside. Fill a large pot with water, salt heavily (it should taste like seawater), and bring to a boil. Add the broccoli spigarello and blanch until bright green and tender, about 2 minutes. Drain, immediately plunge into ice water until cooled, and drain again.

2. In a medium saucepan over medium-low heat, heat the olive oil until shimmering. Add the garlic, cover, and cook until tender but not browned, about 1 minute. Add the broccoli spigarello and chile flakes. Stir slowly to gently reheat. Serve hot with gnocchi or risotto, if desired.

Roasted Brussels Sprouts, Butternut Squash, and Apple with Candied Walnuts (Vegan)

Adapted from Carmen Quagliata,
Executive Chef, Union Square Cafe

TIME: 1¹/₂ hours
YIELD: 2 to 3 servings

FOR THE BRUSSELS SPROUTS:

1¹/₂ cups trimmed, halved
   brussels sprouts
2 cups peeled butternut
   squash, cut into 1-inch
   asymmetrical chunks
2 cups (about 1 large)
   Honeycrisp, Cortland, or
   Granny Smith apple,
   cored and cut into 1-inch
   asymmetrical chunks
1 shallot, cut crosswise into
   ¹/₄-inch slices
2 tablespoons olive oil
5 fresh sage leaves
Salt and freshly ground
   black pepper
¹/₂ tablespoon maple syrup

Carmen Quagliata, the executive chef at Union Square Cafe, is often at the Greenmarket near the restaurant.

In the fall, he is drawn to brussels sprouts, butternut squash, and apples. Cooked with candied walnuts, they make a perfect fall dish.

He cuts the brussels sprouts in half, and the butternut squash and the apples in asymmetrical chunks, and suggests you do not stir the vegetables and fruit as they cook. "You want sharp, roasted edges," he said. "You don't want it fuzzy." Look for the Honeycrisp apple. "It holds its shape and won't turn into applesauce," he said.

The candied walnuts add a sweet, luxurious crunch. If you are in a rush, you can substitute store-bought candied walnuts. But if you have the time, make them yourself. They are fresh, light, and crisp, and have just the right amount of sweetness. You might want to triple the recipe. They can be stored for 3 days, and the oil can be reused. Skim it, refrigerate it, and reuse it when the urge to make candied walnuts sneaks up on you again. To serve the dish as a complete meal, Mr. Quagliata suggests serving it with toasted walnut bread.

1. For the brussels sprouts: Preheat the oven to 375°F. In a large, shallow baking dish, toss the brussels sprouts, butternut squash, apples, and shallot with the olive oil and sage leaves. Season with salt and pepper to taste. Bake without stirring until the vegetables and

{continued}

6 cups vegetable or canola oil,
or as needed for frying

6 ounces walnut halves

2 cups confectioners' sugar

Kosher salt

Walnut bread, for serving
(optional)

apples are wrinkled, slightly brown, and the edges of the squash are beginning to crisp, 45 minutes to 1 hour. Meanwhile, prepare the walnuts.

2. For the walnuts: Place a deep fryer or high-sided saucepan over high heat, and add vegetable or canola oil to come no closer than 3 inches from the top of the pot; when the walnuts are added, the oil will bubble and rise. Heat to 375°F. If using a saucepan, reduce the heat to very low to hold the temperature.

3. In a medium pot over high heat, bring 4 cups of water to a boil. Add the walnuts and boil for 10 seconds. Drain well and immediately toss with the confectioners' sugar. Spread flat on a baking sheet and allow to dry for a few minutes.

4. Have a baking sheet lined with paper towels nearby. Confirm that the temperature of the oil is 375°F, adjusting as needed. Working in batches if necessary, add the walnuts and stir once or twice. Fry until amber-brown, about 30 seconds. Using a wire skimmer or heatproof slotted spoon, remove from the oil and transfer to paper towels. Sprinkle lightly with salt and allow to cool for 5 minutes before handling. May be stored in an airtight container at room temperature for up to 3 days.

5. To serve: Remove the vegetables from the oven, drizzle with maple syrup, and sprinkle with 2 to 3 tablespoons of halved or roughly crumbled walnut pieces. Serve with walnut bread, if desired.

C

Braised Cabbage (Vegan)

Adapted from Floyd Cardoz

TIME: *30 minutes*
YIELD: *3 servings*

1½ pounds savoy cabbage
¼ cup plus 1 tablespoon
  canola oil
2 whole cloves
1 tablespoon black mustard
  seeds
20 fresh curry leaves
1 bay leaf
2 tablespoons finely chopped
  shallot
2 teaspoons finely chopped
  garlic
2 tablespoons peeled julienned
  fresh ginger
½ tablespoon ground turmeric
1 to 2 tablespoons finely
  chopped seeded jalapeño
  pepper
1 cup chopped fresh or
  canned tomato
1½ cups vegetable broth
Kosher salt
Cooked rice, for serving
  (optional)

Floyd Cardoz was the executive chef at Tabla, an Indian restaurant that closed at the end of 2010. One of his favorite dishes is to braise savoy cabbage into beautifully caramelized wedges that rest in a puddle of broth, topped with crunchy black mustard seeds, tomato cubes, and flecks of bright green jalapeño pepper.

1. Cut the cabbage into 6 to 8 wedges, with the widest part no more than 2 inches, leaving the core intact so the wedges will stay together while cooking. Place a heavy skillet, large enough to hold the wedges fairly snugly, over medium heat. Add ¼ cup oil and heat until it shimmers. Add the cabbage, and cook, turning once, until browned on both sides, 2 to 3 minutes a side. Transfer to a plate and set aside.

2. Reduce the heat to medium-low, add the remaining 1 tablespoon oil, and heat until it shimmers. Add the cloves, mustard seeds, curry leaves, bay leaf, shallot, and garlic; cook, stirring, for 1 minute. Add the ginger, turmeric, 1 tablespoon jalapeño, tomato, and broth. Season with salt to taste. If desired, add more jalapeño to taste.

3. Increase the heat to medium-high and bring to a boil. Add the cabbage, fitting it tightly together in the bottom of the pot. Cover, reduce the heat to medium, and braise the cabbage until tender, about 10 minutes, turning it once halfway through cooking. Remove and discard the cloves, curry leaves, and bay leaf. If desired, serve with rice.

Fall Vegetable Cookpot: Braised Red and Green Cabbage (Vegan)

Adapted from Didier Elena, Executive Chef, Adour Alain Ducasse

TIME: *2 hours*
YIELD: *4 servings*

FOR THE CABBAGE:

Salt

2 tablespoons white vinegar

1 large head of red cabbage, cored, 4 intact outer leaves set aside, remaining leaves finely julienned

4 intact outer leaves of a savoy cabbage

4 tablespoons olive oil

1 white onion, thinly sliced

2 cups vegetable broth

1 large napa cabbage, cored, leaves finely julienned

2 teaspoons reduced balsamic vinegar or Saba

3 teaspoons crushed juniper berries

Freshly ground black pepper

Fleur de sel

Didier Elena, the executive chef at Adour Alain Ducasse, makes cabbage rolls that are not the stuff of peasant life, but neither are they hard to make. They simply take time.

His are a duo of balls, one red, one green. The red gets a zap of reduced balsamic vinegar or Saba. The green one does not. The little spheres bake in the oven on a bed of thinly sliced butternut squash, celery root, apple, and pear, and just a splash of broth. Since they are seasoned with a sprinkle of crushed juniper berries, black pepper, fleur de sel, thyme, and lime zest, when you lift the lid of the pot, there is a lovely, delicate aroma.

Note: When you first braise the sliced cabbage, he advises covering the pan with plastic wrap, not the pan's own lid. Many lids rise up a bit in the middle. "If you put a lid on it, the water will rise to the lid and drip to the middle, and the edges will burn," he said. By covering the pot with a flat sheet of plastic wrap, the water will rise and drip evenly. He uses savoy cabbage to wrap the balls, and napa cabbage, for its tenderness, to stuff it. He suggests using the remaining savoy cabbage for coleslaw.

1. For the cabbage: Prepare two large bowls of ice water and set aside. Bring two pots of heavily salted water, each with a tablespoon of white vinegar, to a boil. Add 4 outer leaves of red cabbage to one pot and 4 outer leaves of savoy cabbage to the other. Blanch until tender, about 2 minutes. Remove and plunge into the separate ice baths. Drain and set aside, keeping them separate.

1½ teaspoons whole juniper
berries

1½ teaspoons whole black
peppercorns

1½ teaspoons fleur de sel

1½ teaspoons fresh thyme
leaves

1½ teaspoons finely chopped
lime zest

4 ounces peeled butternut
squash, sliced ¼ inch thick

4 ounces peeled Honeycrisp or
Gala apple, sliced ¼ inch
thick

4 ounces peeled celery root,
sliced ¼ inch thick

4 ounces peeled pear, sliced
¼ inch thick

½ cup plus 2 tablespoons
vegetable broth

2. Place two cast-iron pans over low heat, add 2 tablespoons olive oil to each pan, and heat until shimmering. In one pan combine the julienned red cabbage and half the onion, and sauté until the onion is translucent, 5 minutes. Add 1 cup vegetable broth and cover the pan with plastic wrap. In the second pan, combine the julienned napa cabbage and remaining half onion, and sauté until the onion is translucent, 5 minutes. Add the remaining 1 cup vegetable broth and cover the pan with plastic wrap. Cook both pans of cabbage until the cabbage is tender and the liquid has evaporated, about 25 minutes.

3. When the red cabbage is tender, add the reduced balsamic vinegar or Saba, 1½ teaspoons crushed juniper berries, and pepper and fleur de sel to taste; mix well. When the napa cabbage is tender, add the remaining 1½ teaspoons crushed juniper berries and pepper and fleur de sel to taste; mix well.

4. For assembly: Preheat the oven to 350°F. Place a blanched red cabbage leaf in the palm of your hand and add a quarter of the braised red cabbage in the center. Form a snug ball with the whole leaf as a wrapper. Repeat to make 4 balls of red cabbage. Repeat with the blanched savoy cabbage, using julienned napa cabbage as the filling, to make 4 balls of green cabbage.

5. In a mortar, combine 1½ teaspoons juniper berries, 1½ teaspoons black peppercorns, 1½ teaspoons fleur de sel, 1½ teaspoons thyme, and 1½ teaspoons lime zest. With a pestle, grind the mixture coarsely and set aside.

6. In the bottom of a large covered baking dish, arrange the butternut squash, apple, celery root, and pear so that they slightly overlap at the edges of the dish. Add the 8 balls (alternating red and green), vegetable broth, and ground juniper berries with seasonings. Cook, covered, for 40 minutes. Serve hot.

Cabbage Soup (Vegan)

Adapted from Zoe Feigenbaum, Executive Chef, The National

TIME: 3 hours
YIELD: 8 servings

2 tablespoons olive oil

2 tablespoons minced garlic

1 cup minced or grated onion

1 cup peeled thinly sliced
    carrots

One 28-ounce can peeled
    plum tomatoes in puree

1 cup tomato paste

½ cup tomato ketchup

½ cup dark brown sugar

1 bay leaf

½ cup lemon juice

3 pounds cabbage, tough
    outer leaves, core, and ribs
    removed, and remainder
    sliced into ¼-inch-wide
    ribbons

½ cup golden raisins

Freshly ground (preferably
    medium grind) black pepper

Sour cream (optional)

One of Bess Feigenbaum's legacies to her granddaughter, Zoe Feigenbaum, the executive chef of The National in Manhattan, was a recipe for stuffed cabbage with a sweet-and-sour tomato-based sauce. "There was lots of cabbage in the sauce, and some brown sugar, lemon juice, raisins, tomatoes, and ketchup," said Ms. Feigenbaum.

Ms. Feigenbaum improvised on the recipe from her grandmother, who died in Manhattan in 2009 at the age of ninety. "There was never a written recipe for it," Ms. Feigenbaum said. "It was a Jewish folkloric recipe."

She transformed the sauce into a deeply traditional Jewish cabbage soup.

When I served the soup to three Jewish men, all raised in New York City, it elicited sighs of joy and remembrance.

How tender you want the cabbage, at the very end, will depend on your own taste. Once you add the cabbage, the final simmering may take up to 2 hours before the cabbage is really, really soft.

The soup is vegan; the garnish of sour cream is optional.

1. In a 6-quart pot over medium-low heat, heat the olive oil and add the garlic. Cover and cook until the garlic is tender but not browned, about 2 minutes. Add the onion and sauté until translucent. Add 3 cups water, carrots, whole tomatoes and their puree, tomato paste, ketchup, brown sugar, and bay leaf. Simmer at a lively bubble for 10 minutes, then crush the whole tomatoes with a potato masher or

fork. Continue to simmer until the carrots are tender, about 10 minutes. Remove and discard the bay leaf.

2. Using an immersion blender or working in batches with a stand blender, blend the sauce to make a uniformly coarse mixture; do not puree. Return the sauce to the pot and add the lemon juice, cabbage ribbons, and 3 cups water. Place over medium-high heat and cook at a lively simmer until the cabbage is cooked to taste, from al dente to meltingly soft, 1 to 2 hours. Add 3 to 6 cups water to thin to the desired consistency. Ten minutes before serving, stir in the raisins and a few twists of black pepper. If desired, garnish each serving with a dollop of sour cream.

Cabbage and Mushroom "Lasagna"

Adapted from Marcus Jernmark, Executive Chef, Aquavit

TIME: 2 hours
YIELD: 6 servings

9 tablespoons unsalted
   butter
3 tablespoons plus 1 teaspoon
   unbleached all-purpose flour
2 2/3 cups whole milk
1/4 teaspoon freshly grated
   nutmeg
Salt and freshly ground
   black pepper
1 medium onion, chopped
1 garlic clove, minced
1 pound assorted fresh
   mushrooms (shiitake, oyster,
   porcini, chanterelles,
   cremini), thinly sliced
1 tablespoon finely chopped
   fresh sage
2 pounds napa cabbage,
   12 large leaves removed from
   the head and reserved, the
   remainder chopped into
   rough dice

Marcus Jernmark, the executive chef of Aquavit in Manhattan, serves a cabbage and mushroom lasagna, a golden, bubbling layered dish of sautéed mushrooms, napa cabbage, and thinly sliced potatoes bound with a béchamel sauce and topped with grated Västerbotten or Parmesan cheese.

The dish was inspired by his roots. "My background is Swedish, and I have some French heritage as well," he said. "In Sweden, we eat cabbage, kale, and mushrooms in the fall."

Like most chefs, he likes to work with a trio of different kinds of mushrooms, never just one kind. "Shiitake, porcini, chanterelles, cremini, and oysters are possibilities," he said. "It's a seasonal take on a lasagna, and it's very homestyle."

In a lush kind of way.

1. Preheat the oven to 350°F. In a large saucepan over medium heat, melt 6 tablespoons of the butter. Add the flour, stir for 3 minutes (do not allow to brown), then gradually whisk in the milk, stirring until thickened, 5 to 8 minutes. Stir in the nutmeg and season with salt and pepper to taste. Remove from the heat, allow to cool, and reserve.

2. In a 14-inch sauté pan over medium heat, melt 2 tablespoons of the remaining butter. Add the onion and garlic, and sauté until the onion is translucent. Add the mushrooms, sage, and chopped cabbage, and sauté until fragrant and the cabbage is tender, 10 to 12 min-

½ cup dry white wine

1½ pounds (about 4) Yukon
Gold potatoes, sliced ⅛ inch
thick

1 cup grated Västerbotten or
Parmesan cheese

utes. Add the wine and sauté until it has evaporated. Add the reserved sauce and simmer for 10 minutes. The mixture should be very thick but slightly fluid; if necessary, add a little milk or water. Season with salt and pepper to taste.

3. While the mushroom and cabbage mixture is simmering, pour 6 cups of water into a stockpot and bring to a boil. Add the whole cabbage leaves and blanch for 2 minutes. Drain under cold water and pat dry.

4. With the remaining 1 tablespoon butter, grease a 9 by 9-inch glass baking dish. To assemble the lasagna, line the bottom of the dish with half the cabbage leaves, and top with half the potatoes and half the creamed mushrooms. Repeat the layering of cabbage, potatoes, and mushrooms, and top with the grated cheese. Cover snugly with foil and bake for 30 minutes. Uncover and bake until the top is golden brown, about 20 minutes. Allow to cool for 10 minutes, then serve.

Hungarian Cabbage Strudel

Adapted from Andre Heimann, Executive Chef-Owner, Andre's Café

TIME: 1 hour and 55 minutes
YIELD: 4 servings

8 ounces (2 sticks) unsalted
butter, plus more for
greasing the pan

1 very small head of cabbage
or half a medium cabbage
(about 1 pound), cored and
shredded

½ teaspoon salt

½ teaspoon freshly ground
black pepper

10 sheets phyllo dough,
defrosted

"Americans are not exposed to cabbage," said Andre Heimann, the owner of Andre's Café on the Upper East Side of Manhattan, and of Andre's Hungarian Strudels & Pastries in Forest Hills, Queens. "They know coleslaw."

But in Hungary, "Cabbage is used for soup, for entrées, for stuffed cabbage," said Mr. Heimann. And it's used for cabbage strudel, a richly flavored dish of flaky phyllo wrapped around tender cabbage that has first been baked until it becomes both sweet and savory.

At Andre's Café, the phyllo is so thin that it flutters in a breeze. The burnished strudel is made of only five ingredients: cabbage, phyllo, salt, pepper, and butter. Butter rules. It is a recipe Mr. Heimann adapted from Mrs. Herbst's, a Hungarian bakery on Third Avenue, now vanished.

"We learned it from Mrs. Herbst's," said Mr. Heimann, whose mother, Rose, was a saleswoman there. In 1976, when Mr. Heimann opened his bakery in Queens, he hired a baker and a strudel maker from Mrs. Herbst's. In Queens, his staff makes the phyllo every day and dries it with a fan, so it's "paper-thin," Mr. Heimann said. Making phyllo from scratch is a time-consuming, dying culinary art, he said. "Nobody will do it anymore." At home, he suggests serving the strudel with a cucumber salad or soup.

The difference between Andre's strudel and the recipe for home cooks is the phyllo. For the home cook, the phyllo is store-bought. It will still be crisp, flaky, and golden. It will still crumble into shards. But will it be as ethereal as Mr. Heimann's? Probably not.

1. Heat the oven to 350°F. Lightly butter a large baking pan and spread the cabbage evenly in the pan. Sprinkle with the salt and pepper. Cut up 4 ounces (1 stick) butter into small pieces and sprinkle over the cabbage. Cover with foil, sealing the edges. Bake until tender and golden, 45 to 60 minutes, occasionally lifting the foil and mixing the cabbage, then resealing.

2. Remove from the heat, uncover, and allow to cool to room temperature. (May be stored, covered and refrigerated, for up to 24 hours; use chilled.)

3. Set the oven temperature to 400°F. In a small saucepan, melt the remaining 4 ounces butter. Place a sheet of parchment paper on a work surface with the narrow end closest to you and top with a sheet of phyllo dough. Brush lengthwise (up and down) with a little butter. Top with another sheet of phyllo and brush again with butter. Repeat until all 10 sheets are buttered and stacked.

4. Arrange the cabbage on the top sheet, at the end closest to you, in a thick layer 2 inches deep. Spread evenly to the side edges. With the help of the parchment paper (and rolling as if for sushi in a bamboo roller), roll the phyllo starting at the end with the cabbage. As you work, adjust the parchment paper so that the phyllo is rolled, enclosing the cabbage, without the paper. Brush the top of the roll with butter, place on a baking sheet, and bake until golden, about 40 minutes. Serve hot or warm.

Korean Cabbage Pancake
(Kimchi Pancake)

Adapted from Haksoon Kim, Executive Chef, Kunjip

TIME: 20 minutes
YIELD: 3 pancakes

FOR THE DIPPING SAUCE:

1 tablespoon soy sauce

¼ teaspoon sesame oil

¼ teaspoon vinegar

¼ teaspoon minced scallion

¼ teaspoon sesame seeds

FOR THE PANCAKE:

½ cup flour

½ cup potato starch

1 egg

2 scallions, cut into 1½-inch-
    long pieces

1½ tablespoons garlic,
    thinly sliced

1½ tablespoons Korean red
    pepper powder or ½
    tablespoon cayenne

1 teaspoon salt

1 cup prepared cabbage kimchi,
    cut in 3-inch-long pieces

2 tablespoons kimchi juice

6 tablespoons vegetable oil

When Hae Wha Pak and her partners opened Kunjip, a Korean restaurant in Midtown, she and Haksoon Kim, the executive chef, decided to reinvent the traditional savory pancake. The pancake is usually made with wheat flour and filled with scallions and spicy pickled cabbage (kimchi).

Mrs. Pak's daughter, Christina Jang, who is also an owner of the restaurant, said, "In Korea we have a potato pancake, and my mother found out that the potato pancake is more chewy and stickier, and so she added potato starch" to her New York version.

Not to be confused with potato flour, potato starch is a thickener; it makes Kunjip's pancake similar in texture to a hearty latke.

The pancake is served with a dipping sauce of soy sauce, sesame oil, vinegar, scallions, and sesame seeds.

Ms. Jang said that a kimchi pancake is "a between-meal snack. Drinkers like it at night, street vendors are cooking these and selling them in Seoul, and kids eat it like a slice of pizza." And as in a pizza or an omelet, the pancake is open to infinite variations and improvisation. "You can add hot green pepper or minced zucchini, or as many ingredients as you have at home," Ms. Jang said. "Personally, I like it plain."

1. Make the dipping sauce: In a small bowl, combine the soy sauce, sesame oil, vinegar, scallion, sesame seeds, and ½ tablespoon water. Set aside.

2. In a large bowl, mix the flour, potato starch, and egg until smooth. Add the scallions, garlic, red pepper powder, salt, kimchi, and its juice. Mix well. The batter will be pale pink.

3. Place an 8- or 9-inch nonstick skillet over medium-high heat and add 1 tablespoon vegetable oil. When the oil is hot, pour in one-third of the pancake batter. Fry until golden and crisp, about 3 to 4 minutes. Lift the pancake with a spatula, add 1 tablespoon oil to the pan, and swirl it. Flip the pancake and fry the other side until golden, 2 to 3 minutes. Flip again without adding oil and fry for 1 minute. Flip one more time and fry 1 to 2 minutes. The pancake should be dark gold.

4. Repeat with the remaining batter and oil, making 3 pancakes. Remove to a large round plate and cut each pancake into 6 wedges. Serve with the dipping sauce.

Red Cabbage Salad (Vegan)

*Adapted from Kurt Gutenbrunner, Chef and
an Owner, Wallsé, Café Sabarsky, and Blaue Gans*

TIME: *5 minutes*
YIELD: *4 servings*

6 tablespoons lingonberry
  preserves
¼ cup walnut oil
2 tablespoons sherry vinegar
1 very small head (about
  1 pound) of red cabbage,
  thoroughly cored and very
  thinly sliced
¼ cup walnuts, roasted and
  roughly chopped
Salt and freshly ground
  black pepper
Half an apple, cored and sliced
  into thin julienne
Brown bread, butter,
  and cheese, for serving
  (optional)

Red cabbage, in Kurt Gutenbrunner's view, is underrated. "It's over-looked," he said. "It's not fancy enough."

But sometimes, said Mr. Gutenbrunner, who is the chef and an owner of Wallsé, Café Sabarsky, and Blaue Gans, "you take a cheap product and make something beautiful out of it."

A few years ago he took a traditional Austrian side dish—braised red cabbage marinated in red wine, lingonberries, salt, and spices—and transformed it into a raw salad of finely chopped cabbage and roasted walnuts. He dressed it with walnut oil, sherry vinegar, and lingonberry preserves, and topped it with julienned apple.

The cabbage, slicked with the dressing, is ruby red. The apples are pale yellow or white-green, depending on the variety, and every ingredient is crunchy. But it's the sweet-and-sour lingonberries that make the salad distinctive. As Mr. Gutenbrunner said, "The lingonberries make the salad play."

To build a full dinner around it, he suggested a sour brown bread, like rye, and a cheese like a Cheddar or a soft blue.

"If you are allergic to walnuts, you can use sunflower oil or avocado oil" instead of walnut oil, he said, "and substitute croutons for the nuts, so you have a similar texture."

1. In a mixing bowl, combine the lingonberry preserves, walnut oil, and vinegar. Add the cabbage and walnuts, and mix thoroughly. Season with salt and pepper to taste, and mix again.

2. To serve, divide the salad among four plates. Garnish with the apple. If desired, serve with brown bread, butter, and cheese.

Warm Cabbage and Green Beans

Adapted from Marcus Samuelsson,
Chef-Owner, Red Rooster Harlem

TIME: *2 hours*
YIELD: *4 to 6 servings*

FOR THE SPICED BUTTER:

8 ounces clarified butter
   or ghee
1/2 cup coarsely chopped
   red onion
1 garlic clove, minced
One 2-inch piece ginger,
   peeled and finely chopped
1/2 teaspoon fenugreek seeds
1/2 teaspoon ground cumin
1/2 teaspoon cardamom seeds
1/2 teaspoon dried oregano
1/4 teaspoon ground turmeric
4 whole fresh basil leaves

FOR THE CABBAGE AND
GREEN BEANS

1/2 cup spiced butter (recipe
   above) or 8 tablespoons
   (1 stick) unsalted butter
1 pound cabbage or napa
   cabbage, thinly sliced
   or shredded

Marcus Samuelsson, the chef and owner of Red Rooster Harlem in Manhattan, is a fan of an Ethiopian dish made of warm cabbage and green beans. "It's poor man's cooking," he said. "For fine people, the big pieces of meat and fish came later."

The dish, which tastes even better the second day (and the third), is a complexly seasoned, rich mix of cabbage, green beans, and tomatoes, braised in clarified butter.

The butter is not simple ghee. It is spiced with onion, garlic, ginger, fenugreek, cumin, cardamom, oregano, and basil.

It is just the beginning. Once the vegetables go into the spiced butter, you then add more spices: garlic, mustard seeds, turmeric, berbere, cardamom, ginger, and nigella sativa (also known as black seeds, black cumin, black caraway, and black onion seed). The vegetables braise and the spices do their work, but in a subtle, harmonious way. No spice stands out; all meld.

"In cooking vegetarian meals, it's okay to be a little bit richer, a little bit hotter in temperature than you normally would, " said Mr. Samuelsson, who is Ethiopian by birth; he was adopted by Swedish parents and raised in Sweden. He also adds texture with the crunchiness of the mustard seeds and the black seeds.

At Mr. Samuelsson's home in Harlem, which he shares with his wife, Maya, a model and herself an excellent home cook, the cabbage dish was eaten with injera, the slightly sour, spongy, addictive flatbread that Maya had just brought back from Ethiopia. If injera is not available, rice can be substituted.

1 medium red onion, thinly
sliced

3 cups cherry tomatoes or
5 large tomatoes

7 ounces chopped canned
tomatoes

3 garlic cloves, minced

1 tablespoon mustard seeds

1 tablespoon nigella sativa
seeds

1 teaspoon ground turmeric

1 teaspoon berbere
(available from Kalustyan's
http://kalustyans.com/)
or chile powder

½ teaspoon ground
cardamom, preferably
freshly ground

One 3-inch piece ginger,
peeled and grated

3 cups green beans, trimmed
and cut in half

½ teaspoon salt

Injera (available at Ethiopian
or Eritrean restaurants) or
rice, for serving (optional)

1. For the spiced butter: Melt the butter in a medium saucepan over low heat, and add the onion, garlic, ginger, fenugreek, cumin, cardamom, oregano, turmeric, and basil. Cook for 15 minutes, stirring occasionally. Remove from the heat and let stand until the spices settle, about 10 minutes, then strain through a fine-mesh sieve into a heatproof bowl. May be stored in a tightly covered container for up to 3 weeks.

2. Melt the spiced butter in a 12- to 14-inch sauté pan over medium heat. Add the cabbage and onion, and sauté until the cabbage is wilted, about 5 minutes. Add the cherry tomatoes, chopped tomatoes, garlic, mustard seeds, nigella seeds, turmeric, berbere, cardamom, and ginger. Cook over low heat, stirring occasionally, until soft and fragrant, about 30 minutes.

3. Meanwhile, put 6 cups water in a medium saucepan and bring to a boil. Set aside a bowl of ice water. Add the green beans to the pan, reduce the heat to low, and simmer until tender, 3 to 5 minutes. Drain, plunge the beans into ice water until chilled, then drain again.

4. Fold the green beans into the tomatoes and cabbage. Simmer until the beans take on the flavors of the spiced sauce, about 10 minutes. Adjust the salt to taste. If desired, serve with injera or rice.

Cauliflower Flan (*Cauliflower Sformato*)

Adapted from Adam Weisell

TIME: *2 hours*
YIELD: *Six 4-ounce flans*

FOR THE SFORMATO:

Salt

Half a large head (about
   12 ounces) of cauliflower

1 cup milk, plus 1/4 cup or as
   needed

2 tablespoons butter

2 tablespoons plus
   1 1/2 teaspoons flour

2 large eggs, beaten

1/4 cup grated Parmigiano-
   Reggiano cheese, plus more
   for garnish

Freshly grated nutmeg

Freshly ground black pepper

Unflavored nonstick spray

Cracked or coarse black
   pepper, for garnish

Adam Weisell, the former executive chef of Aurora in Brooklyn, grew up in Rome, where his father worked for the United Nations. His *Cauliflower Sformato*—a savory cauliflower flan studded with a few tiny florets—is "a play on cauliflower and cheese," he said. It is to cauliflower and cheese what a beignet is to an ordinary doughnut.

Because the flan is rich with butter, eggs, cheese, and spices, it is baked in tiny 4-inch-diameter ramekins. Eating one little flan is nearly a complete meal in itself, especially when drizzled with a spoonful of fonduta sauce, a warm melt of heavy cream and Gorgonzola dolce. A salad is the apt accompaniment.

The sformato takes nearly two hours to make. But the upside is this: "It will last three days," Mr. Weisell said. In fact, it is easier to un-mold if you warm it up the next day by reheating it, covered, in a water bath at 400°F for 15 minutes. The sauce takes only a few minutes to make.

It is a lush little thing.

1. Preheat the oven to 350°F. Place a large pot of lightly salted water over high heat and bring to a boil. Cut the half head of cauliflower into quarters, removing the outer leaves and the tougher part of the stem. With a sharp knife, cut the florets into 1-inch pieces, and slice the center stalk thinly.

FOR THE FONDUTA SAUCE
(OPTIONAL):

1/2 cup heavy cream
4 ounces Gorgonzola dolce
   (creamy, sweet Gorgonzola)

2. Reserve a packed 3/4 cup of the florets; add the remaining florets and sliced stems to the boiling water. Boil until tender, 5 to 10 minutes. Drain well and transfer to a blender. Blend, adding 1/4 cup milk, or as needed, to make a very thick, smooth puree. Pour into a large bowl and set aside.

3. In a small pot over medium-high heat, heat 1 cup milk just until steaming. Season with salt to taste. Cover and turn off the heat. In a second small pot over medium heat, melt 1 tablespoon butter, and whisk in all the flour. Cook until thickened, whisking constantly, about 3 minutes. Add the hot milk and whisk constantly to make a thick béchamel, 3 to 5 minutes.

4. Fold the béchamel into the cauliflower puree. Add the eggs, 1/4 cup Parmigiano-Reggiano, a pinch of nutmeg, and salt to taste. In a small sauté pan over medium-high heat, add the remaining 1 table-spoon butter and the 3/4 cup cauliflower florets. Sauté until tender. Season with salt and pepper to taste, and fold the florets into the béchamel mixture.

5. Bring a kettle of water to a boil. Lightly coat the insides of six 4-ounce ramekins with nonstick spray, and fill almost to the top with the flan mixture. Place in a baking dish and add boiling water until it reaches two-thirds up the sides of the ramekins. Cover tightly with a sheet of aluminum foil and bake for 40 minutes. Uncover, and cook about 20 minutes, until the centers are firm yet still jiggle a little. Remove the ramekins from the water and cool to room temperature. Cover and refrigerate overnight or up to 3 days.

{continued}

6. To serve, preheat the oven to 400°F. Bring a kettle of water to a boil. Meanwhile, allow the ramekins to sit at room temperature until no longer chilled. Place in a baking dish and add boiling water until it reaches two-thirds up the sides of the ramekins. Cover tightly with foil and bake until reheated, about 15 minutes. Meanwhile, if desired, prepare the fonduta sauce.

7. For the fonduta sauce: In a small pot over low heat, combine the heavy cream and Gorgonzola dolce. Stir until melted and smooth.

8. To serve: Remove the sformato from the water bath. Run a knife around the inside of a ramekin and place a small plate on top. Invert and remove the ramekin. The sformato should unmold effortlessly. Repeat with the remaining ramekins. Spoon fonduta sauce over each sformato, and sprinkle the top with a little black pepper and grated Parmigiano-Reggiano.

Cauliflower with Almonds, Capers, and Raisins

Adapted from Michael Anthony, Executive Chef, Gramercy Tavern

TIME: *45 minutes*
YIELD: *4 servings*

1 head of cauliflower,
   trimmed of leaves
1½ tablespoons butter
3 tablespoons fresh soft
   bread crumbs
1 teaspoon plus 1 tablespoon
   extra-virgin olive oil
3 tablespoons whole almonds
Salt and freshly ground
   black pepper
2 tablespoons golden raisins
1 tablespoon white
   wine vinegar
1 tablespoon capers,
   rinsed and drained
1 teaspoon finely
   chopped parsley
1 teaspoon finely
   chopped tarragon
1 teaspoon finely sliced chives

When Michael Anthony, the executive chef at Gramercy Tavern, met Mindy Dubin, an artist, in 2004, he discovered that she didn't like cauliflower. It was a stab to his heart and stomach.

So he embarked on what he called the "cauliflower operation," creating at least five dishes solely to woo her. This one—thick golden slices of roasted cauliflower sprinkled lightly with capers, toasted almonds, and raisins plumped in white wine vinegar—was one of the best.

His plan worked: Thanks in part to it, he and Ms. Dubin wed in 2007.

His bride secured, Mr. Anthony decided to put all that vegetable cooking to use at Gramercy Tavern. When he started there in 2006, he had noticed that a signature dish was a grilled vegetable sandwich.

"The sandwich had been there somewhere shy of forever, and a lot of people connected with it," he said; customers saw it "as a go-to source of comfort."

He decided that he, too, wanted to make dishes that customers would not only crave for the moment, but remember. He analyzed the grilled vegetable sandwich and stripped away the bread and the cheese. Not too surprisingly, what ended up on the plate was this cauliflower creation, embellished with a dusting of toasted bread crumbs. "Is there anything more seductive than toasty crunch?" Mr. Anthony asked.

{continued}

1. Preheat the oven to 350°F. Cut the cauliflower from top to bottom in 1-inch slices. Place a large ovenproof skillet over low heat and add 1 tablespoon butter. When it has melted, add the bread crumbs and toss until toasted and golden brown, about 3 minutes. Transfer the crumbs to a plate and wipe out the pan.

2. Return the pan to medium heat and add 1 teaspoon olive oil. Add the almonds and toss until lightly browned, 2 to 3 minutes. Season lightly with salt and pepper to taste. Transfer the almonds to a plate, let cool, and cut each almond into 3 pieces; set aside.

3. Wipe out the pan and return to medium heat. Add the remaining 1 tablespoon olive oil and the cauliflower slices. Sauté until lightly browned on both sides. Transfer the pan to the oven and roast until tender, about 12 minutes. Meanwhile, in a small saucepan over low heat, melt the remaining $1/2$ tablespoon butter and add the raisins, vinegar, and 1 tablespoon water. Simmer until the raisins are plump and soft, about 5 minutes; drain and set aside. In a small bowl, combine the almonds, capers, raisins, parsley, tarragon, and chives. Season with salt and pepper and toss to mix.

4. Arrange the roasted cauliflower on a serving platter. Spoon the almond-herb mixture evenly on top and sprinkle with the toasted bread crumbs. Serve immediately.

Indian Stir-Fried Cauliflower (Vegan)

Adapted from Hemant Mathur,
Executive Chef and a Partner at Tulsi

TIME: *40 minutes*
YIELD: *4 servings*

1 large whole cauliflower,
    cut into 2-inch florets
2 tablespoons canola oil
3/4 teaspoon cumin seeds
1 to 2 Thai bird chiles (about
    1 inch long), seeded and
    finely minced
3/4 teaspoon ground coriander
3/4 teaspoon ground cumin
Small pinch of chile powder
1/3 teaspoon turmeric
Salt
Half a small orange bell
    pepper, cut into 1-inch dice
Half a small red bell pepper,
    cut into 1-inch dice
1 1/2 very large heirloom
    tomatoes or 3 large plum
    tomatoes, cut into 1-inch dice
2 tablespoons chopped
    cilantro
Cooked rice or bread,
    for serving

"This is my favorite northern Indian street food," said Hemant Mathur, the executive chef and an owner of Tulsi, a restaurant in Manhattan. He was speaking of the dish called *gobi taka tin*, or stir-fried cauliflower with peppers and tomatoes.

"*Taka tin* is the sound of the dish cooking, the sound of the metal spoon hitting against the metal pan as the chef keeps the vegetables moving around in the spices and breaking up the too-large pieces of cauliflower."

The chef said he first ate the dish when he was a teenager in Jaipur. Now he eats it once a week for dinner.

"It is very simple," he said. "It is sweet from the peppers and sour from the tomatoes, and it uses not too many spices." One more selling point: its brilliant color.

1. Immerse the cauliflower florets in a bowl of cold water and set aside.

2. Place a large, heavy-bottomed skillet with a lid over high heat and add the oil. When the oil is shimmering, add the cumin seeds and cook, stirring rapidly, until golden brown, about 30 seconds. Add 1 minced chile, the coriander, cumin, chile powder, and turmeric.

3. Drain the cauliflower, add to the skillet, and sauté for 5 minutes, stirring constantly to avoid burning. (If the mixture starts to stick, add

{continued}

1 to 3 tablespoons water.) Season with salt to taste. Stir. Adjust the spiciness to taste, adding part (or all) of the second chile, if desired. Reduce the heat to medium-low. Cover and continue to cook, lifting the lid and stirring occasionally, until the cauliflower is tender, 8 to 10 minutes.

4. Add the orange and red bell peppers, cover, and cook for 2 minutes. Add the tomatoes, cover, and cook for another 2 minutes. Increase the heat to high and cook, uncovered, stirring occasionally, until the tomatoes are soft and most of the liquid has evaporated. Stir in the cilantro and serve immediately. If desired, serve with rice or bread.

Swiss Chard Torta

Adapted from Raffaele Ronca, Executive Chef, Palma

TIME: *1 hour and 15 minutes.*
YIELD: *4 main-course servings*
or 6 appetizer servings

Salt

2 pounds Swiss chard, roughly
chopped, tough stems
discarded

20 cherry tomatoes

4 tablespoons extra-virgin
olive oil

1 Spanish onion, finely chopped

2 garlic cloves, thinly sliced

1/4 cup torn or chopped
flat-leaf parsley

1/4 cup torn or chopped basil

3 large eggs

6 tablespoons freshly grated
Parmigiano-Reggiano
cheese

1 1/2 cups Gruyère cheese,
sliced in rectangles 1/8 inch
thick, 1 inch long, and 1/2 inch
wide

Raffaele Ronca, the executive chef at Palma, offered to make a spectacular Swiss chard torta.

"To me a torta is two inches thick, and it can be sweet or savory," said Mr. Ronca, who grew up in Giugliano, near Napoli. "A grandmother would make it on a special occasion, to welcome someone home," he said. In his family, he especially remembers his mother's escarole torta.

The Swiss chard torta, however, is not his mother's recipe. In 2004, a friend of his, Fedora "Jinx" Cozzi Perullo, a former principal of Stuyvesant High School, made it for him. "I loved it and started making it," Mr. Ronca said. "I think chard is an amazing green. I love the bitterness of it." The chard torta reminded him of his mother's escarole version.

It is a beautiful, deeply flavored, highly textured dish—golden brown on top, dark green within, and studded with red tomatoes.

1. Preheat the oven to 350°F. Bring a large pot of lightly salted water to a rolling boil. Add the Swiss chard and cook until tender, 5 to 10 minutes. Drain thoroughly. Wrap in a towel, and squeeze to remove excess moisture. Unwrap, chop finely, and set aside.

2. Place the cherry tomatoes in a small bowl. Using tongs, squeeze each tomato, crushing it slightly, and discarding as much skin as possible. Set aside.

{continued}

⅓ cup pitted green olives,
  or as needed
⅓ cup pitted kalamata olives,
  or as needed
Freshly ground black pepper
4 tablespoons bread crumbs
2 tablespoons pine nuts,
  lightly toasted

3. Place a 12-inch sauté pan over medium heat, and add 3 tablespoons olive oil, the onion, and garlic. Sauté until soft and golden brown, about 15 minutes. Add the Swiss chard, parsley, and basil. Sauté about 3 minutes. Stir in the cherry tomatoes and remove from the heat. Allow to cool.

4. In a medium bowl, whisk the eggs with 3 tablespoons Parmigiano-Reggiano. Add the Gruyère and whisk to blend well. Add to the Swiss chard and mix well. Add ⅓ cup green olives and ⅓ cup kalamata olives; if desired, up to an additional ⅓ cup olives may be added. Season with salt and pepper, and mix well.

5. With the remaining 1 tablespoon olive oil, grease a shallow 10-inch round baking dish or pie plate. Dust the bottom with 2 tablespoons bread crumbs. Spread the filling in the pan, dust with the remaining 3 tablespoons Parmigiano-Reggiano, and sprinkle with the remaining 2 tablespoons bread crumbs and the pine nuts. Bake, uncovered, until the top is golden brown, about 30 minutes. Serve hot or at room temperature.

Chickpea Stew (*Chana Punjabi*) (Vegan)

Adapted from Heather Carlucci-Rodriguez

TIME: *1½ hours*
YIELD: *4 servings*

1 tablespoon canola oil or
    other vegetable oil
1 medium onion, chopped
2 teaspoons minced garlic
1 teaspoon minced ginger
1 small Thai bird chile, chopped
2 large tomatoes, chopped
1½ teaspoons paprika
1 teaspoon salt, or as needed
1 teaspoon ground coriander
½ teaspoon garam masala
¼ teaspoon turmeric
1 teaspoon freshly squeezed
    lemon juice
Two 15-ounce cans chickpeas,
    drained
2 tablespoons minced cilantro
Cooked rice, for serving
    (optional)

An Indian chickpea stew, *Chana Punjabi* is a plain Jane of a dish: beige beans in a tomato-based spiced sauce, flecked with minced cilantro. Mixed with rice, though, it becomes a soulful meal whose charms are hard to resist.

This version belongs to Heather Carlucci-Rodriguez, who was the chef and owner of Lassi, a 420-square-foot sliver of an Indian cafe with a counter and a few stools in Greenwich Village that has since closed.

Ms. Carlucci-Rodriguez was a pastry chef at L'Impero. In 2004, when she was teaching pastry making at the Institute of Culinary Education in Manhattan, her head was turned.

"One of my students brought me her home cooking," Ms. Carlucci-Rodriguez said. "It was homemade parathas with keema mattar—ground lamb with peas. The flavors were more refined and distinct, and the food wasn't laden with ghee."

She was hooked, and started baking parathas, the hot, thin layered breads, and stuffing them with shredded daikon, potatoes, or cauliflower. She made curries from scratch, caramelizing onions and adding garlic, ginger, and chiles. She whipped up lassis, the fruit and yogurt shakes, with a tablespoon of sugar and a sprinkle of ground cardamom.

In 2005, she opened Lassi. Of the twelve homey dishes on her menu, along with six parathas, her favorite is *Chana Punjabi*.

"When I'm really hungry and need to be satisfied, I always reach for that dish," she said. "It's satisfying. It has a bite to it." It reminds her of her Italian roots. "I'm Sicilian, and in the Sicilian cuisine, the

{continued}

chickpea is used a lot," she said. "There's something earthy and tangy about beans."

1. In a medium saucepan over medium-low heat, heat the oil and add the onion. Sauté until translucent and soft, about 5 minutes. Add the garlic, ginger, and chile, and sauté until soft and fragrant, about 3 minutes. Add the tomatoes and 1/4 cup water. Cover and cook until the tomatoes are very soft, about 5 minutes, then remove from the heat.

2. Puree the mixture in a blender or food processor until smooth. Return to the pan and place over medium heat. Add the paprika, 1 teaspoon salt, the coriander, garam masala, turmeric, and lemon juice. Add the chickpeas and bring to a boil, then reduce the heat to low.

3. Cover and simmer until the sauce is thick and the chickpeas are soft, 45 minutes to 1 hour. Stir the pan about every 10 minutes, adding water as needed (up to 1 1/2 cups) to prevent burning. When ready to serve, the sauce should be thick. If necessary, uncover the pan and allow the sauce to reduce for a few minutes, stirring frequently, until it reaches the desired consistency. Stir in the cilantro, adjust the salt as needed, and serve with cooked rice, if desired.

Thai Green Curry Vegetables (Vegan)

Adapted from Drew Spangler Faulkner

TIME: 1 hour
YIELD: 4 servings

One 13.5-ounce can coconut
milk (do not shake can)
½ cup vegetable stock
4 teaspoons soy sauce
4 teaspoons palm sugar
or brown sugar
4 tablespoons Thai green
curry paste, such as Thai
Taste, Maesri, and Thai
Kitchen, none of which
have shrimp or fish paste,
or more as needed.
½ cup diced (½-inch) onion
⅔ cup diced (½-inch) red bell
pepper
⅔ cup diced (½-inch)
zucchini or other summer
squash

Drew Spangler Faulkner, a cooking teacher at L'Academie de Cuisine, in Bethesda, Maryland, makes a Thai green curry that is a kind of Asian comfort food. The sauce, made creamy with coconut milk and mildly spicy with the curry paste, is flavorful yet soothing. The vegetables, which are simply dropped into the sauce and gently simmered for about 12 minutes, turn out tender, not soggy. The vegetables blend slightly, but when you bite into the eggplant or the sweet red pepper, the vegetable—and its identity—are intact. As Ms. Faulkner has conceived this popular dish, it is startlingly simple.

It is a recipe that she distilled after traveling in Thailand in the late '80s, and also working with Thai chefs at the CIA Greystone campus in St. Helena, California, in the mid-'90s. She makes her own green curry paste, but the recipe calls for store-bought pastes. Although some green curry pastes contain fish or shrimp paste, she has found three that do not: Thai Taste, Maesri, and Thai Kitchen.

1. Open the can of coconut milk without shaking it. Spoon 6 tablespoons of the coconut cream from the top of the can into a medium saucepan. Pour the remaining contents of the can into a medium bowl and mix well. In another medium bowl, combine the vegetable stock, soy sauce, and palm or brown sugar. Stir until the sugar is dissolved.

{continued}

2/3 cup diced (1/2-inch) peeled
sweet potato
2/3 cup sliced bamboo shoots,
rinsed and drained
1 cup green beans, trimmed
and cut into 1 1/2-inch lengths
2/3 cup diced (1/2-inch) Asian
eggplant
1 lime
8 large basil leaves, cut into
thin chiffonnade
Cooked jasmine rice, for
serving (optional)

2. Place the saucepan of coconut cream over medium-high heat until it begins to bubble. Add the curry paste and reduce the heat to medium-low. Stir constantly until very fragrant, about 3 minutes; adjust the heat as needed to prevent burning. Taste for spiciness. Add up to two tablespoons of curry paste to taste. Add the onion, red pepper, zucchini, sweet potato, bamboo shoots, green beans, and eggplant. Stir until the vegetables are hot, 2 to 3 minutes. Stir in the coconut milk, bring the mixture to a boil, and reduce the heat to low. Simmer, uncovered, until the vegetables are tender, about 10 minutes.

3. Add the soy sauce mixture and a generous squeeze of fresh lime juice to taste; you may use the juice of an entire lime. Stir and mix well. Add up to 1/4 cup water if the curry seems too thick.

4. To serve, place the curry in a warm serving bowl and garnish with the basil chiffonade. If desired, serve over jasmine rice.

Corn Chowder

Adapted from Patricia Williams, Executive Chef,
Smoke Jazz & Supper Club-Lounge

TIME: 1¹/₂ hours
YIELD: 4 servings

6 ears of corn

2 onions, diced

4 tablespoons unsalted butter
 or olive oil

¹/₂ cup heavy cream

2 teaspoons salt

Freshly ground black pepper

4 sprigs micro greens,
 like pea shoots, for garnish

When fresh sweet corn comes into season, Patricia Williams, the executive chef at New York's Smoke Jazz & Supper Club-Lounge, creates a light, delicious corn chowder that is very simple to make. "I go by the season first, start with one ingredient, and then build up the flavor," she said.

The base of the soup is a naturally sweet, thin corn stock made from the cob and one diced onion. While the stock simmers, she slowly sautés a second diced onion, so as not to take on any color. Then she sautés the kernels, adds the strained broth and cream, and simmers the soup. Toward the end, she pours half the soup into a blender, then returns it to the pot for a final minute of reheating. The pale soup, speckled by the whole corn kernels, is deceptive. It is thin, yet deeply flavored. It is a soup to be made while corn is at its sweetest.

1. Using a sharp knife, cut the kernels off the ears of corn and set aside, reserving the cobs. In a large saucepan, combine the cobs, 1 diced onion, and 8 cups water. Place over high heat to bring to a boil, then reduce the heat to medium. Cover and cook for 20 minutes. Turn off the heat and allow to steep for an additional 30 minutes.

2. While the corncobs are steeping, place a large saucepan over medium-low heat and add the butter or olive oil. Add the remaining diced onion and sauté until translucent and soft, about 20 minutes;

THE OCCASIONAL VEGETARIAN   69

do not allow to take on any color. Add the corn kernels and sauté until slightly translucent, about 5 minutes. Remove from the heat and set aside.

3. When the stock has finished steeping, strain it, discarding the cobs and onions. Add 6 cups stock to the pot of corn kernels; discard any remaining stock or reserve for another use. Return to medium heat and simmer until the corn is soft, about 2 minutes. Add the heavy cream, reduce the heat to low, and cook for 15 minutes.

4. Remove half the soup and allow to cool until no longer steaming when stirred. Hot soup cannot be pureed in a blender because the aeration makes the top blow off and the hot soup spews all over. Working in batches, puree the cooled soup in a blender until the kernels are partly broken or smooth, depending on your preference, then return to the pot, reheating gently if necessary. Season with salt and a few grinds of black pepper. Divide among four bowls and garnish with the micro greens.

Corn Fritters

Adapted from Djoko Supatmono, Executive Chef, Satay Junction

TIME: *40 minutes*
YIELD: *4 appetizer portions*

FOR THE DIPPING SAUCE:

1/3 cup Thai sweet chili
    sauce

1/3 cup Bango or other
    kecap manis (sweet soy
    sauce, available at Asian
    markets)

FOR THE FRITTERS:

4 ears of corn, kernels cut
    from cob, or one 15.25-ounce
    can corn, drained

2 garlic cloves, minced

1 tablespoon red bell pepper,
    julienned into pieces 1/2 inch
    long and 1/8 inch wide

In Indonesia, corn fritters, a popular street food, are served from morning until night. "Corn is as sweet in Jakarta as it is here," said Djoko Supatmono, the executive chef at Satay Junction, an Indonesian restaurant in Manhattan.

Mr. Supatmono uses canned corn to make his fritters, but in the height of corn season, fresh corn can also be used.

1. For the sauce: In a small bowl, combine the sweet chili sauce and kecap manis. Mix and set aside.

2. For the fritters: In a large bowl, combine half the corn kernels, garlic, red bell pepper, nutmeg, black pepper, and egg. Mix well. Place in a blender and process at medium speed until pureed. (Variations: For a smooth fritter, add all the corn to the blender; for a very crunchy fritter, reserve all the corn for step 3.)

3. Transfer back to the bowl; add the sugar, cornstarch, rice flour, shallot, and reserved whole corn kernels. Mix well and season with salt to taste.

{continued}

½ teaspoon grated nutmeg

½ teaspoon freshly
   ground black pepper

1 large egg

½ teaspoon sugar

2 tablespoons cornstarch

2 tablespoons rice flour

1 tablespoon finely
   chopped shallot

Salt

Vegetable oil

4. In a wok or a deep frying pan over high heat, add the vegetable oil to a depth of 1½ to 2 inches. Heat to 350°F. Working in batches, scoop up the corn mixture 1 tablespoon at a time and add to the hot oil; be careful not to crowd the pan. Fry until golden brown, 1½ to 2½ minutes a side; fresh corn may take slightly longer to brown than canned. Drain and place on paper towels. Serve with the dipping sauce.

Corn Pudding

Adapted from Lois Freedman,
President, Jean-Georges Management

TIME: 40 minutes
YIELD: 3 servings

8 ears of corn, husked
1 tablespoon butter
Salt
Cayenne pepper
Half a lime

Lois Freedman is now the president of Jean-Georges Management in New York City. But she was once a cook with Jean-Georges Vongerichten at the four-star Lafayette restaurant.

In 1994, she discovered the simplest, most delicious way to make corn pudding. She grates fresh corn kernels directly into a cast-iron pan, puts it in the oven without any seasonings, lets the milk released by the corn thicken, and removes it 20 minutes later, golden and lightly caramelized around the edges. Only then does she season it, and only lightly: a bit of butter, a sprinkle of salt and cayenne, and the juice of half a lime. Mix. Serve.

When asked why she doesn't add the butter, salt, cayenne, and lime juice before she bakes the corn, Ms. Freedman said that if she seasoned the corn ahead of time, she couldn't control what the final dish would taste like. The seasonings might be too intense for what is a very delicate, pure-tasting dish.

"The sweetness of the corn caramelizes it," she said. "I made it for Jean-Georges, and he loved it, and every year, we put it on the menu at Jo-Jo's and the Mercer in Manhattan, and at my own restaurant, Cucina in Woodstock."

1. Preheat the oven to 350°F.

2. Place a box grater on a medium cast-iron pan and finely grate each ear of corn directly into the pan. Discard the cobs.

{continued}

3. Spread the milky corn evenly across the pan, and bake until the edges and top are golden brown and the corn milk has thickened, 20 to 30 minutes.

4. Remove from the heat, and transfer the corn and any liquid to a bowl. Add the butter, and season to taste with salt, cayenne pepper, and a squeeze of lime juice. Mix well and serve.

Crepes (*Crespelle*)

Adapted from Albert Di Meglio

TIME: *55 minutes*
YIELD: *10 crepes, 5 servings*

FOR THE CREPES:

1/3 cup chestnut flour

1/4 cup pastry flour

1 teaspoon salt

Finely grated zest of 1 lemon

1/2 cup milk

3/4 cup plus 2 tablespoons
   heavy cream

3 large eggs

4 tablespoons butter,
   melted, plus more for
   greasing pans

FOR THE FILLING:

1 large egg

8 ounces sheep's milk ricotta
   or other ricotta

8 ounces herb-and-garlic
   Boursin

In 2001, when Albert Di Meglio was about to become the executive chef at Osteria del Circo in Manhattan, the owner, Sirio Maccioni, asked him to travel through Tuscany first on an eating tour.

There, Mr. Di Meglio tasted a Monte Bianco, a dessert that begins with a tart shell, then a layer of airy chestnut mousse flecked with candied, crumbled chestnuts and a topping of whipped cream. He was also invited to visit Mr. Maccioni in Montecatini, where his wife, Egidiana Maccioni, made a *crespelle*, an Italian version of a crepe.

The delicate golden *crespelle* was filled with ricotta, a bit of lemon zest, a twist of black pepper, and a scattering of Parmigiano-Reggiano. It was baked for 10 minutes, then topped with toasted pine nuts and brown butter.

What made it Tuscan was that the batter, instead of being made entirely of regular flour, was made with half chestnut flour; the latter imparted a faint sweetness to the otherwise savory dish.

The *crespelle*, Mr. Di Meglio said, "found a small place in my heart." It also found a place on the menu of Olana near Gramercy Park, which has since closed. While there, he tweaked the filling by mixing Boursin with the ricotta "for a little bit more flavor." He also changed the regular flour to pastry flour to make the crepe softer.

"I love *crespelle* as a one-course meal," he said. "It's enough to get you full. Salad and two *crespelle*, I'm good to go."

{continued}

½ cup finely grated
  Parmigiano-Reggiano
  cheese
Finely grated zest of 1 lemon
Salt and freshly ground
  black pepper

FOR THE GARNISH:
¼ cup pine nuts
4 tablespoons butter

1. For the crepes: In a mixing bowl, combine the chestnut flour, pastry flour, salt, and lemon zest; set aside. In another bowl, combine the milk, cream, eggs, and 4 tablespoons melted butter; whisk until smooth. Add the milk mixture to the flour mixture and whisk until smooth.

2. Butter a 10-inch nonstick or stainless-steel skillet. Place over a medium-high flame until well heated, 1 to 2 minutes. Add ¼ cup batter to the center of the pan, spreading it into a thin disk. Cook until golden brown underneath, 2 to 3 minutes. Flip and cook an additional minute. Place on a warm plate and cover with a towel to keep warm. Repeat, stacking the crepes as they are ready, to make 10 crepes.

3. For the filling: In a mixing bowl, combine the egg, ricotta, Boursin, Parmigiano-Reggiano, and lemon zest. Season to taste with salt and pepper.

4. For the garnish: Place a dry 10-inch skillet over medium heat and add the pine nuts. Stir until the nuts are lightly browned, about 3 minutes, then transfer to a plate. Add the butter to the pan and raise the heat to medium-high. Allow the butter to brown, 3 to 5 minutes. Remove from the heat, stir in the nuts, and set aside.

5. For assembly: Preheat the oven to 350°F. Lightly butter a baking sheet. Spread a thin layer of filling evenly over the entire surface of each crepe. Fold the crepe twice to form a triangle. Place on the baking sheet. Repeat with the remaining filling and crepes. Heat in the oven until hot, about 10 minutes.

6. To serve, place 2 or more *crespelle* on a plate and garnish with the browned butter and pine nuts.

E

E.A.T.'s Egg Salad Sandwich

Adapted from Eli Zabar

TIME: _30 minutes_
YIELD: _2 sandwiches_

8 large eggs
⅓ cup Hellman's Mayonnaise
Salt and freshly ground
   black pepper
1 tablespoon chopped
   fresh dill
4 slices bread

Eli Zabar's E.A.T., the food emporium on Third Avenue and 80th Street, has an egg salad that seems to be fresher, tastier, and richer than most others.

The question is why.

I called Mr. Zabar and he revealed the secret.

To four hard-boiled eggs, he also adds four hard-boiled egg yolks, along with Hellman's Mayonnaise, salt, pepper, and chopped fresh dill.

It's those four extra yolks, whipped.

When he told me the recipe, I said, "That's it? That's all?"

"Yes," he said. "That's it."

It was in 1975 that he came upon what he calls the platonic ideal of the egg salad sandwich, which was to eliminate half the egg whites. That was the period when he was into pure simplicity, to get to the essence of the "egginess" of an egg salad sandwich.

He succeeded. The recipe remains unchanged thirty-five years later.

1. Put the whole eggs in a medium saucepan and add cold water to cover. Place over high heat and bring to a boil. Reduce the heat to medium-low and simmer 10 minutes. Drain under cold water until cooled.

{continued}

THE OCCASIONAL VEGETARIAN   79

2. Peel the eggs. On a chopping board place 4 whole eggs and 4 yolks; reserve the remaining 4 whites for another use. Chop the eggs and yolks moderately finely, or to taste.

3. In a medium bowl, gently and quickly mix the chopped eggs and yolks, mayonnaise, and salt and pepper to taste. Add the fresh dill and mix once more.

4. Divide the egg salad between 2 slices of bread. Spread evenly, top each with a slice of bread, and serve.

Egg Lemon Soup

Adapted from John Fraser, Chef-Owner, Dovetail

TIME: *25 minutes*
YIELD: *4 servings*

Salt

1 cup orzo

5 cups vegetable broth

4 large eggs

¼ cup fresh lemon juice,
  or as needed

3 to 4 teaspoons extra-virgin
  olive oil (optional)

1 teaspoon minced parsley

1 teaspoon minced dill

1 teaspoon minced mint leaves

Freshly ground black pepper

John Fraser, chef and owner of Dovetail restaurant in Manhattan, has a Greek mother, and he can whip up an egg lemon soup in twenty minutes that is creamy and perky. Sprinkled with chopped parsley, dill, and mint, it has the taste of springtime, even on a cold winter day.

The secret of making the soup smooth and not curdling the egg is to watch the temperature of the ingredients. He heats the broth and then removes it from the heat, letting it cool to very warm or hot but definitely not boiling. He whisks the egg and lemon juice thoroughly, adds a cup of the hot broth very, very slowly to the soup, whisking continuously, and brings the temperature of the egg mixture up to that of the broth.

Then he returns the egg-broth mixture to the pot of broth and heats the soup over low heat. What gives the soup some body is, of course, the orzo.

1. Bring 4 cups lightly salted water to a boil in a large saucepan. Stir in the orzo. Cook until tender, about 8 minutes. Drain and set aside.

2. Heat the vegetable broth in a medium pot over medium heat until steaming but not boiling. Remove from the heat and set aside.

{continued}

3. Crack the eggs into a mixing bowl. Add ¼ cup lemon juice and whisk until completely blended. While whisking vigorously, very slowly add 1 cup hot stock to the eggs to bring them up to the temperature of the broth. Add the egg/stock mixture to the rest of the soup, and adjust the lemon juice and salt as needed.

4. Return the soup to low heat, add the orzo, and whisk until thoroughly heated but not boiling, about 4 minutes. To serve, ladle into bowls and if desired, drizzle each with a bit of olive oil. Garnish with a sprinkling of parsley, dill, mint, and black pepper.

Egg White Frittata with Leeks
(*Frittata Bianca ai Porri*)

Adapted from Nick Anderer, Executive Chef, Maialino

TIME: 25 minutes
YIELD: 1 to 2 servings

2 tablespoons plus
  2 teaspoons olive oil
1 tablespoon butter
1 very large leek, white part
  only, sliced into thin rounds
1 teaspoon fresh thyme leaves
Salt and freshly ground
  black pepper
8 ounces egg whites (from
  about 5 large eggs)
3 tablespoons grated pecorino
  cheese
½ cup baby arugula
  or other salad green
¼ cup mizuna leaves
  or other salad green
Half a lemon,
  for squeezing juice

Danny Meyer, the chief executive officer of the Union Square Hospitality Group, which owns Eleven Madison Park, The Modern, and Maialino, among other restaurants, has a favorite breakfast.

It is the frittata bianca—or egg white frittata—with sautéed leeks and a sprinkle of pecorino, topped with a salad of baby arugula and mizuna, created by Nick Anderer, the executive chef of Maialino.

So, here's a Q and A with Mr. Meyer on the frittata:

Q: Was this dish the creation of the chef or a request of yours?

A: I think I once mentioned to Nick that it would be nice to have one egg white option on the menu, and he responded by coming up with something that is so incredibly delicious—you forget you're actually eating something so healthy!

Q: Why do you like it so much?

A: I love that it comes with a barely dressed arugula and mizuna salad atop, and that each bite delivers ultimate flavor satisfaction. Because there is almost no fat or carbohydrates in the frittata, I know I'm going to feel light and ready to be productive when I'm back at work.

Q: How often do you eat it?

A: Everyone with whom I have morning business meetings now wants to do them at Maialino for breakfast, so I have the Frittata Bianca at least two or three times per week. I'll be having one tomorrow morning.

{continued}

1. Preheat the oven to 350°F. Place a 7-inch nonstick skillet over medium heat, add 2 tablespoons olive oil and the butter, and heat until bubbling. Add the leek and sauté until it begins to soften, about 5 minutes. Add the thyme, season with salt and pepper to taste, and cook for 1 more minute.

2. In a small mixing bowl, whisk together the egg whites and 2 tablespoons of pecorino. Add to the skillet and gently stir together with the leeks for 1 minute to scramble them gently. Scrape down the sides of the pan.

3. Transfer the skillet to the oven and bake until the center of the frittata stiffens (check by gently shaking the pan) and it is fully cooked, about 7 minutes. Transfer to a plate and sprinkle with the remaining 1 tablespoon of pecorino

4. In a mixing bowl, combine the arugula and mizuna. Add the remaining 2 teaspoons of olive oil and a squeeze of fresh lemon juice. Toss to mix, place on top of the frittata, and serve.

Steamed Eggs à la Harbin Restaurant

Adapted from "Chinese Home Cooking" by Elaine Louie and
Julia Chang Bloch for the Organization of Chinese American Women (1985)

TIME: 40 minutes
YIELD: 4 servings

2 cups vegetable broth,
   at room temperature
1 teaspoon cornstarch
4 large eggs
Freshly ground white
   or black pepper
1 teaspoon plus 2 tablespoons
   vegetable oil
3 scallions, chopped
5 large dried shiitake
   mushrooms, soaked until
   softened, squeezed dry,
   stems trimmed and
   discarded, thinly sliced
¼ cup fresh or frozen peas
¼ cup garlic chives, ends
   trimmed, cut in 1-inch
   lengths
½ teaspoon sugar
1 tablespoon soy sauce
Cooked rice, for serving

When Eva Chang was a young woman growing up in Shanghai, steamed egg custard with sautéed Chinese mushrooms, peas, and scallions appeared on the lunch or dinner table at least twice a month. In the 1940s her family fled the chaos of China and moved to San Francisco, where she became the owner and executive chef of the Harbin Restaurant from 1967 to 1990. She still cooks for her family, and one recipe in particular evokes childhood memories.

This silky, quivering custard dish is found in many areas of China—in Beijing, Guangdong, Chengdu—and also in Japan, where it is known as *chawan mushi*. Some cooks add vegetables or seafood to the custard before steaming it. Others steam the custard and make the savory topping separately.

The trick to getting a silken custard is to add cold or room-temperature broth to the eggs when you beat them. Never add hot broth because it will begin to cook the eggs. When you first beat the eggs, you can do so until they are frothy. But when you add the broth, beat gently so that the eggs do not foam. You want a smooth surface before you add the eggs into the steamer.

1. Bring several inches of water to boil in the bottom of a large steamer. In a small bowl, combine 3 tablespoons vegetable broth with the cornstarch; mix well.

{continued}

2. Place the eggs in a shallow 1½- to 2-quart baking dish and beat until foamy. Add the remaining vegetable broth, a dash of white or black pepper, and 1 teaspoon oil. Beat again gently until well blended. Allow any foam to subside until the surface is completely smooth.

3. Place the dish in the steamer, cover, and lower the heat to medium. Steam until a knife inserted into the eggs comes out clean, 20 to 25 minutes. Meanwhile, in a wok over medium heat, add the remaining 2 tablespoons oil and heat until shimmering. Add the scallions and stir-fry 2 to 3 minutes. Add the mushrooms, peas, garlic chives, sugar, and soy sauce. Stir-fry 2 to 3 minutes. Add the cornstarch mixture and stir-fry 1 minute.

4. When the eggs are ready, pour the mushroom mixture over the eggs. If desired, serve over rice.

Eggplant Caponata Crostini (Vegan)

Adapted from David Seigal, Executive Chef,
The Tangled Vine Wine Bar & Kitchen

TIME: *45 minutes*
YIELD: *4 appetizer servings*

5 tablespoons extra-virgin
olive oil

1 Spanish onion, finely
chopped

2 to 3 garlic cloves, thinly
sliced

1 eggplant (about 3/4 pound),
cut into 3/4-inch dice

Salt and freshly ground
black pepper

3 tomatoes, cut into 3/4-inch
dice

1/2 cup golden raisins

1/3 cup chopped capers

About 1/4 baguette, sliced
diagonally into eight
1/2-inch-thick rounds,
or other crusty bread
slices

Aged balsamic vinegar,
for sprinkling

David Seigal, the executive chef at The Tangled Vine Wine Bar & Kitchen in Manhattan, makes a caponata that works as a crostini, on top of toasted coarse bread, or as a sauce for pasta. What he remembers from his childhood, when his mother made it, was that at the end, she always sprinkled it with a few drops of precious, aged balsamic vinegar at least ten years old.

1. Place a large skillet or sauté pan over medium-low heat. Add 1 tablespoon olive oil and the onion, and sauté until softened, 5 to 6 minutes. Add the garlic and continue to sauté until soft and golden, about 10 minutes. Transfer to paper towels to drain.

2. Wash the skillet and return to medium-high heat. Add 3 tablespoons olive oil and allow to heat until shimmering. Working in batches, if necessary, add a single layer of eggplant and toss to coat in the oil. Fry, stirring frequently, until tender and evenly browned, 5 to 10 minutes. Transfer to paper towels to drain, and season to taste with salt and pepper.

3. Wash the skillet and return to medium heat. Add the remaining 1 tablespoon olive oil and tomatoes. Sauté until the tomatoes are tender but have not lost their shape and almost all the liquid has evaporated.

{continued}

1 to 2 basil leaves, sliced into
  chiffonade
Fleur de sel, Maldon salt,
  or other flaky sea salt

4. In a large bowl, combine the onion mixture, eggplant, tomatoes, raisins, and capers. Toss gently to mix well. Season with salt and pepper to taste.

5. To serve, toast the sliced bread and top with a large spoonful of the caponata mixture. Sprinkle with a few drops of vinegar, and garnish with basil chiffonade and a few grains of flaky sea salt.

Eggplant and Roast Tomatoes Gratin

Adapted from Michael Scelfo, Executive Chef,
Temple Bar and Russell House Tavern

TIME: 1¹/2 hours
YIELD: 4 servings

FOR THE BREAD CRUMBS:

¹/2 cup grated pecorino cheese

1 cup panko (Japanese bread crumbs)

¹/2 teaspoon salt

¹/4 teaspoon freshly ground black pepper

3 tablespoons extra-virgin olive oil

2 teaspoons minced parsley

FOR THE EGGPLANT AND TOMATOES:

1 cup red grape or teardrop tomatoes

1 cup yellow grape or teardrop tomatoes

14 basil leaves, roughly chopped

¹/4 teaspoon red pepper flakes

Michael Scelfo, the executive chef at both the Temple Bar and the Russell House Tavern in Cambridge, Massachusetts, invented this variation on eggplant parmigiana a few years ago.

It was a dish born of desperation.

His twins, Joshua and Mae, were then preschoolers and his son Andrew was a newborn. As busy as Mr. Scelfo is, he cooks for his family on Sunday and Monday nights. One night, he wanted to make eggplant parmigiana, a dish he had grown up with in Merrick, New York, where his maternal grandmother, Rosemary Heyen, who was Italian, made it on many Sundays for supper.

As he was making the dish, he realized he had no time to fry the eggplant, so he just cut the eggplant into cubes and tossed them with fresh grape tomatoes, fresh basil, parsley, olive oil, pecorino, mozzarella, tomato puree, spices, and panko. His toss-with-your hands version of the classic dish is significantly less greasy. "When you fry the eggplant, it takes on a lot of oil, and when you use bread crumbs as a layer, it tends to act as a sponge, in a not good way," he said.

At home, he serves it once a week, and at the Temple Bar, it rotates on the vegetarian menu. It is a simple and tasty dish.

1. For the bread crumbs: In a medium bowl, combine the pecorino, panko, salt, pepper, olive oil, and parsley. Mix well until the crumbs are evenly coated with oil. Set aside.

{continued}

1 teaspoon salt

1/2 teaspoon freshly ground
   black pepper

1 1/4 cups tomato puree

5 large garlic cloves, peeled
   and thinly sliced

2 to 2 1/4 pounds eggplant,
   peeled and cut into 1-inch
   cubes

1/3 cup extra-virgin olive oil,
   plus more for drizzling

1 cup fresh whole milk buffalo
   mozzarella or other
   mozzarella cheese, grated
   or finely chopped

2. For the eggplant and tomatoes: Preheat the oven to 375°F. In a large bowl, combine the red tomatoes, yellow tomatoes, basil, red pepper flakes, salt, black pepper, tomato puree, garlic, eggplant, and 1/3 cup olive oil. Add half of the bread crumb mixture. With your hands or two spoons, gently mix the vegetables and bread crumb mixture until thoroughly combined.

3. Pour into a 9 by 13-inch baking dish and top with the remaining bread crumb mixture. Sprinkle the mozzarella over the top. Bake, uncovered, until the eggplant is tender and the top is lightly browned, 45 to 60 minutes; if after 30 minutes the top is browning too rapidly, cover the dish with foil for the remaining cooking time. Remove from the oven and let rest for 10 minutes before serving. Drizzle olive oil to taste over each serving, if desired.

Empadas
(Portuguese Stuffed Pastries)

Adapted from Luisa Fernandes, Chef, The Best Chocolate
Cake in the World, and Executive Chef, Nomad

TIME: 1¹/₂ hours
YIELD: 6 servings

2 tablespoons olive oil

1 cup finely chopped
    red onion

1 garlic clove, finely chopped

1 cup finely diced (¹/₃-inch)
    zucchini

1 cup finely diced yellow
    squash

1 cup finely diced eggplant

¹/₂ cup finely diced tomatoes

2 teaspoons finely chopped
    fresh thyme

2 tablespoons finely chopped
    parsley

1 tablespoon red wine
    vinegar

Salt and freshly ground
    black pepper

Luisa Fernandes, consulting chef at The Best Chocolate Cake in the World in Brooklyn and executive chef at Nomad in Manhattan, makes a savory empada—a Portuguese stuffed pastry—that is similar to a ratatouille wrapped in puff pastry. She sautés eggplant, tomatoes, squash, onions, and garlic, and once the vegetables are cooled, she tucks them into puff pastry in muffin tins and bakes them until they are golden. "It's a very old Portuguese recipe that's served for lunch with a salad," said Ms. Fernandes, who makes it for The Best Chocolate Cake in the World.

1. Preheat the oven to 400°F. In a large skillet over medium heat, heat the olive oil until shimmering. Add the onion and garlic, and sauté until translucent, about 5 minutes. Add the zucchini, squash, and eggplant, and sauté until they are tender but have not lost their shape, about 10 minutes. Add the tomato, thyme, and parsley, and cook until the tomatoes soften but do not lose their shape, about 5 minutes. Add the red wine vinegar. Season to taste with salt and pepper.

2. In a small bowl, mix 1 tablespoon flour with 3 tablespoons water. Mix well and add to the vegetables. Cook for 3 minutes, stirring. Transfer to a baking sheet to cool until no longer steaming, then place in the refrigerator to chill, uncovered, for 15 minutes.

{continued}

1 tablespoon all-purpose
   flour, plus additional as
   needed
One to two 14 by 16-inch
   sheets puff pastry
1 tablespoon butter
   or nonstick cooking spray
1 large egg, beaten
Salad, for serving

3. Place one sheet of puff pastry on a lightly floured work surface. Using a 3½- to 4-inch-diameter cookie cutter or cup, cut out 6 disks. Using a 1½-inch cookie cutter, cut out 6 more disks. Roll all the disks out to a ⅛-inch thickness.

4. Butter or spray a 6-cup muffin pan with 3-inch diameter cups. Place a large disk in each of the holders; the dough should overlap the holder by about an inch or more. Add one-sixth of the chilled vegetables to each cup. Place the small circle of pastry on top of the vegetables, and fold over the edges of the larger circle to fully enclose the empada. (It may be possible to pinch together the edge of the large disk of dough without using the smaller disk.) Brush the tops with the beaten egg.

5. Bake the empadas until golden brown, 25 to 40 minutes. Using a knife, gently loosen them from the muffin tins. Transfer to plates and serve hot. If desired, serve with a salad.

Enchiladas (Vegan)

Adapted from Ayinde Howell, Caterer,
former Executive Chef, JivamukTea Café

TIME: 1 hour and 15 minutes
YIELD: 2 to 3 servings

FOR THE SAUCE:

¼ cup safflower or other
    vegetable oil

Half a medium onion, diced

2 garlic cloves, minced

1 jalapeño pepper, seeded
    and diced

1½ tablespoons ground
    cumin

1½ tablespoons chili powder

3 tablespoons all-purpose
    flour

8 ounces canned organic
    tomato sauce

Sea salt

FOR THE FILLING AND ASSEMBLY:

¼ cup safflower or other
    vegetable oil

1 pound firm tofu, drained
    and loosely crumbled

Ayinde Howell was born a vegan baby to Afrocentric vegan parents. His name, he explained, is Yoruba for "We gave praise, and he came."

He grew up in Tacoma, Washington, where his parents had a restaurant called Hillside Quickie, which made vegan sandwiches using tofu and tempeh. The Howells now have four restaurants in the Tacoma-Seattle area. Mr. Howell has never eaten meat. "I once ate egg by accident in some Thai food and was sick for two days," he said.

In 2006, he moved to Brooklyn, where he has taken the family's vegan passion and expanded it. In Manhattan, he was the executive chef at the JivamukTea Café, the restaurant within the influential Jivamukti yoga studio in Manhattan. Now he caters and consults, and makes vegan food that is remarkably tasty and robust.

When he makes the enchiladas in tomato sauce, the crisp dark brown nuggets of firm tofu become toothsome impersonators of hamburger. A carnivore could be fooled.

1. For the sauce: In a small saucepan over medium heat, heat the oil until shimmering. Add the onion, garlic, and jalapeño. Sauté until the onion is translucent, about 5 minutes. Add the cumin, chili powder, and flour, whisking until browned and thickened. Slowly stir in ¾ cup water and the tomato sauce, mixing well. Reduce the heat to low and simmer for 15 minutes. Season to taste with salt. Remove from the heat and keep warm.

{continued}

Half a medium onion,
   finely diced
Half a red bell pepper,
   finely diced
2 garlic cloves, minced
1 jalapeño pepper, seeded and
   finely diced
1 cup coarsely chopped
   cilantro leaves
1½ tablespoons ground cumin,
   or more to taste
1½ tablespoons chili powder,
   or more to taste
2 tablespoons soy sauce
Sea salt
Six 7-inch corn tortillas
Green salad, for serving

2. For the filling and assembly: Preheat the oven to 375°F. In a medium skillet over medium heat, heat the oil until shimmering. Add the tofu and cook until brown and somewhat crispy and its liquid has evaporated, stirring from underneath to prevent sticking, 10 to 15 minutes.

3. Once the tofu looks brown and cooked on all sides, add two-thirds of the onion and half of the red bell pepper. Stir, and add the garlic, jalapeño, cilantro, cumin, and chili powder; mix well. Add the soy sauce and mix well. Season to taste with the sea salt. Sauté until the onion and red bell pepper begin to soften, 5 to 10 minutes. Add 1 to 2 tablespoons water if the mixture seems parched, but it should be dry, and the tofu should resemble crisped, browned bits of meat.

4. While the tofu mixture is cooking, wrap the tortillas tightly in aluminum foil and place them in the oven for 10 minutes. Remove, keeping them wrapped, and set aside.

5. In a shallow 9 by 7-inch casserole (or large enough to hold the enchiladas snugly in one layer), add one-third of the sauce to coat the bottom of the casserole. Unwrap the hot tortillas and place one in the sauce to coat it, then turn it over so that it is coated on both sides. Add one-sixth of the filling and roll the tortilla tightly. Place it, seam side down, on the sauce. Repeat to make 6 filled tortillas. Pour the remaining sauce on top of the tortillas and sprinkle with the remaining uncooked onion and red bell pepper. Bake until the sauce is bubbling, about 15 minutes. Serve, if desired, with a green salad.

Endive Cheese Tart

Adapted from Roland Caracostea

TIME: *2 hours and 45 minutes*
YIELD: *6 to 8 servings*

FOR THE DOUGH:

½ cup confectioners' sugar

1 cup all-purpose flour

Pinch of salt

4½ tablespoons unsalted
   butter, at room temperature,
   cut into small pieces

1 large egg

FOR THE FILLING:

3 pounds small Belgian
   endives, trimmed of brown
   edges

8 tablespoons unsalted butter

½ cup granulated sugar

½ pound Époisses cheese

A long train ride. Hungry travelers. Strangers exchanging tales about favorite foods.

From this experience, Roland Caracostea, a graphic designer in Manhattan, acquired a recipe that warms his memory—and his appetite.

It was December 2008. Mr. Caracostea, who was born and raised in Paris, and his wife, Rodica Prato, an illustrator, who was born in Bucharest, were sharing a compartment on a train from Dijon, France, to Rome with a couple from Burgundy. Mr. Caracostea has forgotten their names but not the conversation.

The train, which did not have a café car, was running six hours late. "Nobody was carrying sandwiches; we had skipped lunch, and we were hungry," said Mr. Caracostea, who is a third-generation vegetarian. "The conversation started to slide toward food, and we were talking about tarte Tatin," the classic French apple tart.

The Frenchwoman gave him an idea. "She mentioned doing it with vegetables instead of fruit, and to add some cheese," such as Époisses from Burgundy, creamy, strongly flavored, and expensive ($20 a half pound). Mr. Caracostea took note. Later on his trip, when he found himself in a kitchen in Paris, he tried the tart, first with leeks, then eggplant, and finally Belgian endive, which worked the best.

{continued}

"It's the combination of the slight bitterness of the endive, the sweetness of the caramelizing process, and the richness of the cheese that makes it delicious."

Back home in New York he makes the tart, but only about once a month. "It's very rich," he said. "You have to give your liver time to absorb all that fat."

1. For the dough: In a mixing bowl, combine the sugar, flour, and salt. Add the butter and mix with a pastry cutter or two knives until it resembles large crumbs. Add the egg and mix with a fork until it forms a mass. Shape into a disk and cover with plastic wrap. Refrigerate for 2 hours.

2. Meanwhile, prepare the filling: Fill the bottom of a steamer with 1½ inches of water, place over high heat, and bring to a boil. Add the endives and steam until just tender, about 20 minutes depending on the size. Transfer to a colander and allow to drain for 20 minutes.

3. Place a 9½-inch flameproof baking dish or cast-iron skillet over medium heat. Melt the butter and add the sugar, stirring until dissolved. Reduce the heat to low and add the endives in a circular pattern, tips meeting in the center, or other attractive pattern (which will be visible when the tart is finished).

4. Allow the endives to cook over low heat until the liquid is reduced to a caramel on the bottom of the dish and the endives are golden brown (but not burned) on the underside, 45 minutes to 1 hour. Meanwhile, preheat the oven to 350°F.

5. When the endives are cooked, remove the pan from the heat. Cover the endives evenly with slices of Époisses. Remove the dough from the refrigerator and roll out into a circle large enough to cover and slightly overhang the top of the pan. Place the dough on top of the Époisses; do not try to adjust it once placed.

6. Trim the excess dough from the sides. Perforate in a few places with a sharp knife and bake until the dough is golden brown, 20 to 30 minutes. Remove from the oven. Place a large plate on top of the pan. Invert, gently removing the pan. Serve hot or warm.

Braised Endives with Blood Oranges, Sicilian Pistachios, and Ricotta Salata

Adapted from Jordan Frosolone, Chef, Hearth

TIME: *40 minutes*
YIELD: *2 servings*

FOR THE GARNISH:

2 tablespoons toasted bread
crumbs

½ teaspoon finely grated
orange zest

¼ teaspoon minced garlic

1 teaspoon finely chopped
parsley

FOR THE ENDIVES:

4 endives, halved lengthwise

Salt and freshly ground
black pepper

2 tablespoons butter

3 tablespoons extra-virgin
olive oil

1 cup Verdicchio or
other white wine

Jordan Frosolone, the chef de cuisine at Hearth in Manhattan, is a fan of endive.

"I think endive is an underused vegetable," he said. "People think it's bitter, but bitterness can become desirable."

He made it seductive by braising it with blood oranges (other kinds can be used) and topping it with pistachios and ricotta salata. "Endive is inherently bitter, and blood oranges will balance it," he said. "But how to make it richer and heartier? I added the meatiness of pistachios and the richness of the cheese."

1. For the garnish: In a small bowl, mix together the bread crumbs, orange zest, garlic, and parsley; set aside.

2. For the endives: Season the endives with salt and pepper. In a large sauté pan over medium-high heat, melt the butter with the olive oil. Place endives in the pan, cut side down. Once the endives start to brown lightly, about 5 minutes, add the wine and reduce by three-quarters, another 4 to 5 minutes. As the wine begins to reduce, test the endives for tenderness. Once the endives are tender, remove and transfer them to a plate. Pat dry, cover, and set aside.

1½ cups blood orange
  or other orange juice
2½ teaspoons sugar
1 tablespoon shelled
  pistachios
6 blood orange or other
  orange segments
4 thin shavings ricotta salata
  (½ ounce total)

3. When the wine is reduced, add the orange juice and sugar. Turn up the heat and reduce to a thick, shining syrup, stirring frequently. Lower the temperature to medium-high, add the pistachios and orange segments, and heat for 1 minute.

4. Uncover the endives, and transfer to two warmed plates. Garnish with the bread crumb mixture. Pour the orange syrup with the pistachios and oranges over the endives. Top with thin shavings of ricotta salata and serve.

G

Almond Grape Gazpacho (Vegan)

Adapted from Anthony Sasso, Chef de Cuisine, Casa Mono

TIME: *30 minutes,
plus 2 hours chilling*
YIELD: *4 to 6 servings
(about 6 cups)*

FOR THE GAZPACHO:

3 large garlic cloves

2 cups diced stale bread,
crusts removed

2 cups peeled, fried, and
salted Marcona almonds,
or whole blanched
almonds

1 cup white seedless grapes,
halved

1 cup red seedless grapes,
halved

Salt

1½ cups extra-virgin olive oil

1½ to 2 tablespoons sherry
vinegar

When Anthony Sasso was growing up in Woodstock, New York, "Soups were something that you ate to warm up, a recovery food," he said. If someone in the family had a bad cold, a soup was made with a stock simmered with beef bones or a few chicken legs and a handful of vegetables. As for cold soups, Mr. Sasso said no thanks.

In 2006, he went to Spain for a year to live and cook. In a town called Palafolls in Catalonia, he ate the first cold soup he liked. It was a white gazpacho: almonds, garlic, bread, grapes, olive oil, sherry vinegar, and water—blended into a rich, subtle summer soup.

"It's like drinking almonds, olive oil, and grapes instead of eating them," said Mr. Sasso, who is now the chef de cuisine at Casa Mono near Gramercy Park.

In Spain, gazpachos arrive on the table along with three to four little bowls filled with the same chopped ingredients blended in the soup. The white gazpacho is topped with sliced red and green grapes, whole fried and salted Marcona almonds, scallions, croutons, and a splash of vinegar—a salad atop a soup.

1. For the gazpacho: Place the garlic cloves in a small pan of cold water over high heat. When the water comes to a boil, strain the garlic and chill until needed. Cover the stale bread cubes with water and allow to sit until soft, about 10 minutes.

{continued}

FOR GARNISH AND SERVING:

Extra-virgin olive oil,
   as needed

1/4 cup diced bread

Salt

1/2 cup mixed red and white
   seedless grapes, cut into
   small dice

1/4 cup peeled, fried, and
   salted Marcona almonds,
   or whole blanched almonds

1 scallion, thinly sliced
   diagonally

Almond oil or extra-virgin
   olive oil, for drizzling

Sherry vinegar, as needed

2. Squeeze all the water from the bread and put the bread into a blender with the almonds, grapes, and garlic cloves. Season with a bit of salt and puree until the mixture is very smooth, almost like mashed potatoes; if necessary, drizzle in a bit of water to help the mixture to puree.

3. Place 1 cup ice-cold water in a measuring cup. Place the olive oil in another cup. With the blender running, slowly drizzle in both liquids simultaneously through the opening in the blender top. The gazpacho will turn very smooth and silky. Add 1 1/2 tablespoons vinegar or more, if desired. Adjust the salt to taste. To thin the soup, if desired, add 1 to 3 tablespoons cold water, 1 tablespoon at a time. Transfer to a covered container and refrigerate until very cold, about 2 hours.

4. For garnish and serving: Preheat the oven to 400°F. Drizzle oil over the diced bread and sprinkle with salt. Spread on a baking sheet and bake until browned, 5 to 8 minutes. Transfer to a small bowl and add the grapes, almonds, and scallion. Add a drizzle of oil and a small sprinkling of vinegar and salt. To serve, ladle the gazpacho into four chilled soup plates. Add the garnish and drizzle with more oil.

H

Persian Herb Frittata

Adapted from Nasim Alikhani

TIME: *2 hours*
YIELD: *4 large appetizers*

½ cup barberries or dried
  cranberries
1 cup chopped parsley
  (about 4 ounces)
1 cup chopped cilantro
  (about 4 ounces)
1 cup chopped scallions, white
  part only (about 4 ounces)
⅔ cup chopped romaine
  lettuce (about 6 large
  leaves)
4 large eggs
2 teaspoons kosher salt
2 teaspoons freshly
  ground black pepper
½ cup olive oil
½ cup walnuts,
  coarsely chopped
Greek yogurt, for serving
  (optional)

This beautiful, verdant Persian-style frittata is made from a recipe that at first glance looks ridiculous. It's not the list of ingredients, which sound fresh and lovely with heaps of parsley, cilantro, scallions, and lettuce. Nor is it the first three steps that involve simply chopping, whisking, and cooking for 10 minutes.

It's step 4, which calls for cooking one side of the frittata 40 minutes, then flipping it over and cooking the other side 40 more minutes.

Eighty minutes to make a frittata?

I picked up the phone and called Nasim Alikhani, the Iranian caterer who created the recipe, and said, "Forty minutes a side? Is this a typo?"

"No," she said, laughing. "Come and watch me make it."

In her Greenwich Village loft she made the frittata, explaining that in the interminable 80 minutes that it cooks (enough time to do the laundry, pay the bills, and walk the dog), several things happen. The vegetables give up their moisture, the frittata shrinks in height by two-thirds, and the outside becomes a slightly crisp, dark golden brown—without burning.

The final result is burnished on top, dark green within, and studded with red barberries and crunchy walnuts. Ms. Alikhani served ripe, seedless watermelon as an appetizer. Then, for the frittata, she produced a dollop of Greek yogurt.

{continued}

1. In a small bowl, soak the barberries in cold water for 20 minutes. Using a sharp knife, finely chop the parsley, cilantro, scallions, and romaine lettuce; combine in a large mixing bowl.

2. In a medium mixing bowl, combine the eggs, salt, and pepper. Whisk just until frothy. Drain the barberries, making sure to discard any small stones.

3. Place an 11-inch skillet over medium heat. Add ¼ cup and 2 tablespoons of the olive oil and heat until shimmering. Add the beaten eggs, barberries, and walnuts to the chopped greens. Mix well and pour into the skillet, spreading it evenly. Cover the pan and cook until set, about 10 minutes.

4. Uncover the skillet and divide the frittata into 4 wedges, separating them from one another slightly so that the liquid from the frittata can evaporate. Reduce the heat to low and cook, uncovered, until the underside is browned, about 40 minutes.

5. Turn the frittata over, one wedge at a time. Drizzle the remaining 2 tablespoons olive oil inside the edge of the skillet and between each wedge. Continue to cook, uncovered, until the underside is browned and the frittata is compact and crisp on both sides, an additional 40 minutes. Serve hot or at room temperature, with yogurt on the side, if desired.

Leek Tart with Oil-Cured Olives

Adapted from Katy Sparks and owned by Radish

TIME: *1 hour*
YIELD: *6 small servings*

FOR THE RICOTTA BASE:

1/2 cup whole milk ricotta
 cheese
1 large egg yolk
3 tablespoons olive oil
1/4 cup sour cream
Salt and freshly ground
 black pepper

FOR THE PASTRY:

One 14-ounce package Dufour
 or other all-butter puff
 pastry

FOR THE TOPPING:

2 tablespoons unsalted butter
2 to 4 leeks, white and light
 green parts only, cut
 diagonally into 1/3-inch-wide
 slices (to make a total of
 2 cups)

When Katy Sparks, a restaurant consultant and the former executive chef of Quilty's in Manhattan, was developing a menu for Radish, a take-out place in the Williamsburg neighborhood of Brooklyn, she created a leek tart with oil-cured olives. In her usual fashion, like many chefs, she uses store-bought frozen puff pastry for the tart shell. "I love puff pastry, but because I've never been a great baker, I like help," she said. "We buy Dufour puff pastry."

Mike Ciardi, the chef at Radish, used a knife to score a narrow 1/4-inch border on the pastry to define the edge of the tart. He then used the knife to make a crisscross scoring on the middle of the square of pastry.

"The scoring breaks the strands of dough," he said, "and it will puff where it's not scored." When it came out of the oven, he used a fork to gently poke the puffed middle to allow the steam to escape. Then he let the pastry cool for 10 minutes to become fairly crisp. When the pastry was cool, he added the cooked filling, put the tart into the oven, and baked it until the cheese bubbled and the edges were golden brown.

1. For the ricotta base: Preheat the oven to 375°F. In a bowl, combine the ricotta with the egg yolk and olive oil; whisk until well blended. Stir in the sour cream and season with salt and pepper

{continued}

½ teaspoon fresh thyme
   leaves
Salt and freshly ground
   black pepper
1 egg yolk, beaten
1 cup grated Gruyère cheese
12 oil-cured pitted black olives,
   torn or cut in half

2. For the pastry: Cut the pastry into six 4-inch squares and lightly score a border about ¼ inch from the edge. Lightly score a crisscross pattern on the inside of the square. Place on a baking sheet and bake until puffed and lightly browned, 10 to 20 minutes. Remove from the oven and poke the center with a fork to allow steam to escape. Let cool 10 minutes.

3. For the topping: While the pastry is cooling, place a medium sauté pan over medium heat. Melt the butter, add the leeks and thyme, and sauté until the leeks are soft and lightly caramelized, 10 to 15 minutes. Season with salt and pepper to taste; set aside.

4. Brush the edge of the puff pastry with the beaten egg yolk. Spread the ricotta base over the scored area of the pastry and sprinkle evenly with the Gruyère. Top with the leeks and olives. Bake until the edges are golden brown and the cheese is bubbling, 10 to 14 minutes. Serve hot.

Kalustyan's Lentil Soup (Vegan)

Adapted from Arpiar Afarian, Executive Chef, Kalustyan's

TIME: *1 hour and 10 minutes*
YIELD: *6 to 8 servings*

½ cup red lentils, rinsed and drained

¼ cup long-grain sweet (glutinous) rice, rinsed and drained

¼ cup Kalijeera baby basmati rice, rinsed and drained

3 teaspoons kosher salt

1 teaspoon Osem or Telma brand onion soup and seasoning mix (see Note)

1 teaspoon Osem or Telma brand mushroom soup and seasoning mix (see Note)

1 teaspoon Osem or Telma brand vegetable soup and seasoning mix (see Note)

Kalustyan's, a New York shop famous for its 4,000 products from all over the world, also offers prepared food. One of its most popular is the lentil soup made with glutinous rice, baby basmati rice, and white kidney beans and flecked with cilantro and fried onions, said Aziz Osmani, one of the owners.

Mr. Osmani said the shop uses three kosher powdered bouillon flavors—onion, mushroom, and vegetable—for the broth. The brands are either Osem or Telma, which the chef, Arpiar Afarian, uses interchangeably. The final garnish, the fried onions, is not some time-consuming culinary chore. Kalustyan's sells bags of fried onions, imported from Holland, which, Mr. Osmani said, can keep in a plastic bag or a covered container for six months, either in the refrigerator or a cool place where the temperature never goes above 50 degrees. The soup, without the cilantro and fried onions, can be frozen for up to three months.

1. In a large soup pot, combine the lentils, sweet rice, and baby basmati rice. Add 10 cups water, salt, and the onion, mushroom, and vegetable soup and seasoning mixes.

{continued}

1 cup drained canned white
  kidney beans
1/2 cup extra-virgin olive oil
1/2 cup lightly packed cilantro
  leaves
1/2 cup fried onions (see Note)

2. Place over high heat and bring to a boil. Skim and discard any foam that rises to the top. Reduce the heat to low and simmer, uncovered, for 40 minutes.

3. Stir in the white kidney beans and olive oil, mixing well. Simmer, stirring, until the beans are heated through and the oil has blended with the soup, about 3 minutes.

4. When ready to serve, add the cilantro and fried onions. Mix well for about 1 minute. Serve hot.

NOTE: Available from Kalustyan's, www.kalyustans.com, 800-352-3451. Osem and Telma brands are kosher.

M

Braised Chinese Mushrooms and Baby Bok Choy (Vegan)

Adapted from Elaine Louie and Julia Chang Bloch

TIME: 45 minutes, plus soaking time for dried mushrooms
YIELD: 2 servings

1 teaspoon Lee Kum Kee
(see Note) or other
vegetarian stir-fry sauce,
or vegetarian mushroom-
flavored oyster sauce,
which has no oyster extract

1 tablespoon soy sauce

1½ teaspoons sugar

1 teaspoon sesame oil

½ cup vegetable broth

1 teaspoon rice wine or
dry sherry

2 tablespoons vegetable oil

14 Chinese dried mushrooms,
soaked until softened,
stemmed, and squeezed dry,
or fresh shiitake mushrooms,
stemmed

This lovely dish of glossy braised Chinese mushrooms on a bed of blanched baby bok choy is typically Shanghainese. The success of the dish depends on the quality of the mushrooms. The best ones are large, thick, and meaty, and have beautifully marked caps. It is often served at banquets but can just as easily be served at home.

1. In a small bowl, combine the stir-fry sauce, soy sauce, sugar, sesame oil, vegetable broth, and rice wine or sherry. Mix well and reserve.

2. Fill a large pot about three-quarters full of water and place over high heat to bring to a boil. Meanwhile, in a skillet large enough to hold all the mushrooms in one snug layer, heat the vegetable oil over medium heat until shimmering. Add the mushrooms and stir-fry for 2 minutes. Add the reserved sauce and reduce the heat to low. Cover and simmer for 20 minutes, turning the mushrooms over once or twice. If the pan becomes dry, add 1 to 2 tablespoons water.

3. In a small bowl, combine the cornstarch with 2 teaspoons water and mix well. Add to the mushrooms. Stir gently for 30 seconds, until the mushrooms are glossy. Cover and turn off the heat. Add the baby

{continued}

1 teaspoon cornstarch

14 baby bok choy

2 scallions, white part only, minced

Cooked rice, for serving (optional)

bok choy to the boiling water and blanch until crisp-tender, about 1½ minutes. Drain well and arrange on a platter with the leaves pointed toward the center. Place the mushrooms in the center and garnish with the minced scallions. If desired, serve with rice.

NOTE: Lee Kum Kee Stir-Fry Sauce is available at http://www.amazon.com/Lee-Kum-Vegetarian-Stir-fry-Sauce/dp/B000VS4NTK.

Mushroom and Daikon Soup (Vegan)

Adapted from Anita Lo, Executive Chef-Owner, Annisa

TIME: 30 minutes
YIELD: 4 servings

3 dried shiitake mushrooms

4 dried porcini mushrooms

1 tablespoon vegetable oil

½ small onion, thinly sliced

1 garlic clove, finely chopped

¼ cup Shaoxing wine or
  dry sherry

1 piece kombu, rinsed
  (optional)

8 ounces mixed fresh
  mushrooms, cleaned and
  sliced

¼ cup mushroom or regular
  soy sauce

¾ cup daikon, peeled and cut
  into small cubes, or silken
  white tofu, cut into small
  cubes

Anita Lo, the executive chef and owner at Annisa in Greenwich Village, made a mushroom soup a few years ago that was inspired by the colors of late autumn. It had acorn squash, acorn jelly, and warm shades of brown, gold, and orange. "I was working in earth tones," she said.

She adapted her recipe for spring, resulting in a clear soup of mushrooms and daikon (or tofu). The broth is gently flavored with garlic, onions, soy sauce, Shaoxing wine, and kombu, Japanese seaweed. There's much to chew on.

"I wanted the mushrooms to stand on their own," she said. "And if you buy really delicious mushrooms, everything else supports and makes the whole better." Ms. Lo, who is Chinese-American, said the inspiration for the soup is cross-cultural. "I've never eaten a Chinese mushroom soup, and I don't know that I've had a clear Japanese mushroom soup, but there's a classic miso soup with mushrooms and kombu in it," she said.

"Mushrooms and sherry are classic ingredients together, and Shaoxing wine is very much like sherry," she said. "Kombu adds a depth of flavor, a roundness."

For the fresh mushrooms, generic white button mushrooms work perfectly well if more exotic mushrooms like shiitake, cremini, or oyster are not available.

Ms. Lo serves the soup with a side dish of brown rice, dotted with edamame.

{continued}

Salt and freshly ground
  black pepper
Lemon juice (optional)
4 pinches of chopped scallion
  greens, for garnish

1. Place the shiitake mushrooms in a small bowl; cover with hot water and set aside. Place the porcini mushrooms in a separate bowl; cover with hot water and set aside. Heat the oil in a medium saucepan over medium-low heat. Add the onion and sauté until translucent. Add the garlic and sauté until fragrant, about 1 minute.

2. Add the Shaoxing wine or sherry and reduce by half. If planning to use mushroom soy sauce, add 5 cups water. If planning to use regular soy sauce, add 4²/₃ cups water plus ¹/₃ cup soaking water from the porcini mushrooms. Drain the porcini mushrooms of the remaining water and add to the pan. Add the kombu, if using.

3. Bring to a full boil, reduce the heat to low, and remove and reserve the kombu. Drain the shiitake mushrooms and discard the stems. Slice the caps and add to the pan. Add the fresh mushrooms and soy sauce. Cut the kombu into bite-sized pieces and return to the pan. Add the daikon and simmer until softened, 3 to 5 minutes. If using tofu, simmer only until heated, about 30 seconds.

4. Season to taste with salt and pepper and, if desired, a touch of lemon juice. To serve, divide among four warmed soup bowls and garnish each with a pinch of scallion greens.

Mushroom and Leek Potpie

Adapted from Yoel Cruz, Executive Chef, North Square Restaurant

TIME: 2 hours
YIELD: 2 servings
  (2 individual potpies)

4 tablespoons olive oil

1 garlic clove, finely chopped

3 leeks, white and pale green
  parts only, trimmed and
  sliced into rings

1 cup mixed, thinly sliced
  cremini, oyster, shiitake,
  or other mushrooms

Salt and freshly ground
  black pepper

1 tablespoon butter

1 tablespoon flour

1 cup whole milk

1 cup vegetable broth

1 carrot, cut into 1/3-inch cubes

1 red potato, cut into 1/3-inch
  cubes

1 celery stalk, diced

1/2 teaspoon minced fresh
  oregano leaves

When a potpie comes out of the oven, it should have a puff pastry crown, high, rounded, golden, and gleaming.

Yoel Cruz, the executive chef of North Square Restaurant, makes a simple hearty vegetable potpie with potatoes, carrots, leeks, and chickpeas. I adapted his recipe, deleting the chickpeas and adding sautéed mushrooms. I also tripled the amount of leeks he had suggested.

I used one-quart ceramic soufflé dishes, 3 1/2 inches deep. Once I mixed the vegetables with the hot béchamel sauce, I removed them from the heat and let them cool, so that there wouldn't be a lot of heat that might prevent the puff pastry from rising.

The store-bought Dufour puff pastry did what it was supposed to do. It puffed, nearly two inches above the dish.

1. Preheat the oven to 350°F. Place a skillet over medium heat and heat 2 tablespoons olive oil until shimmering. Add the garlic and leeks and sauté until soft, 6 to 8 minutes. Transfer to a baking sheet and set aside.

2. Return the unwashed pan to medium heat and add the remaining 2 tablespoons olive oil. Add the mushrooms, and sauté until soft and they have given up much of the liquid, about 8 minutes. Add to the baking sheet and lightly toss to mix with the leeks. Season with salt and pepper to taste; set aside.

{continued}

½ teaspoon minced fresh
   thyme leaves
1 teaspoon ground cumin
One 14-ounce package Dufour
   or other all-butter puff
   pastry
1 egg, beaten, for egg wash

3. In a medium saucepan over medium heat, melt the butter. Add the flour and whisk vigorously until golden but not browned, 3 to 5 minutes. Add the milk and whisk until thickened. Add the vegetable broth, leeks, mushrooms, carrot, potato, and celery. Add the oregano, thyme, and cumin. Mix well and season with salt and pepper to taste. Remove from the heat and spread across a baking sheet to cool until no longer steaming, about 10 minutes, then refrigerate until completely cool, another 10 minutes.

4. Divide the vegetable mixture between two 1-quart ceramic soufflé dishes about 6 inches in diameter and 3½ inches deep. Cut the puff pastry into two 8-inch circles; reserve the excess pastry for another use. Brush the edge of each pastry round with the egg wash, then invert and place on the dish, pressing the edge lightly to seal and being sure the pastry does not touch the filling. Brush the tops of the pies with the remaining egg wash. Place the dishes on a baking sheet and bake until the pastry is golden, 25 to 40 minutes. Serve immediately.

Mushrooms in Lettuce Wraps (Vegan)

TIME: *20 minutes*
YIELD: *4 servings*

FOR THE SAUCE:

2 tablespoons soy sauce

1 tablespoon red wine or
other vinegar

1 tablespoon red wine or
dry sherry

1 1/2 teaspoons sugar

1 teaspoon freshly ground
black pepper

1 teaspoon cornstarch

FOR THE FILLING:

16 medium to large Chinese
or Japanese dried
mushrooms, about 2 inches
in diameter, soaked in warm
water until softened, about
45 minutes

2 tablespoons vegetable oil

This delicate dish of finely diced mushrooms and vegetables served in lettuce cups is an adaptation of a Cantonese banquet dish: minced squab, an expensive and very small bird, served in lettuce. At home, a cook might make a thriftier but nevertheless tasty version using chicken.

This recipe substitutes Chinese or Japanese mushrooms—dried ones, reconstituted—and firm tofu for the meat. The mushrooms have a texture similar to meat, and the tofu is a small donation of protein.

It is a handheld dish. Take lettuce with leaves that are round and cuplike, like Bibb, Boston, or iceberg; dab on a bit of hoisin sauce sparingly so as not to overwhelm the flavors; and then top with spoonfuls of the diced mushrooms and vegetables. Wrap and eat.

1. For the sauce: In a small bowl, whisk together the soy sauce, vinegar, wine, sugar, and pepper. In another small bowl, stir together the cornstarch with 1 tablespoon water. Set the bowls aside.

2. For the filling: Drain the mushrooms, trim the tough stalks, and finely dice the mushrooms; there should be about 1 1/2 cups. Place a large wok over high heat and add the oil. When the oil is hot, add the mushrooms, celery, carrots, and scallions. Stir-fry until the celery and carrots are crisp-tender, about 45 seconds. Add the soy sauce mixture and stir for 20 seconds. Add the cornstarch mixture and stir until thickened, about 30 seconds.

{continued}

4 celery stalks, strings removed with a vegetable peeler, finely diced (to make 1 cup)

3 carrots, peeled and finely diced (to make 1 cup)

4 scallions, white and green parts, trimmed and minced (to make 3/4 cup)

2 ounces firm tofu, finely diced

1 teaspoon dark sesame oil

2 to 3 tablespoons lightly toasted pine nuts

TO SERVE:

8 to 12 whole Bibb, Boston, or iceberg lettuce leaves

Hoisin sauce, as needed

3. Add the tofu and toss gently, being careful not to break up the tofu. Add the sesame oil and toss again. Transfer to a serving bowl and sprinkle with the pine nuts.

4. To serve, place the bowl of mushroom filling alongside a platter of lettuce leaves and a small bowl of hoisin sauce. Spread about 1/4 teaspoon hoisin sauce in the center of each lettuce leaf and add 2 tablespoons mushroom mixture. Roll up the leaf and eat with your fingers.

Fragrant Mushroom Spring Rolls, Wrapped in Lettuce Cups

Adapted from Jean-Georges Vongerichten, Spice Market

TIME: 1 hour
YIELD: 4 appetizer servings

FOR THE DIPPING SAUCE:

½ cup sambal oelek

½ cup honey

⅓ cup fresh lemon juice

¼ cup rice wine vinegar

2 teaspoons salt

FOR THE MUSHROOM FILLING:

1 stick butter (8 tablespoons),
  cut into 1-inch cubes

½ tablespoon minced garlic

1 pound oyster or other
  mushrooms, stemmed,
  sliced ½ inch thick

¾ pound shiitake
  mushrooms, stemmed,
  sliced ½ inch thick

¼ teaspoon minced green
  Thai bird chile

Salt

Around 2003, Jean-Georges Vongerichten was in Singapore, where he ate a fragrant mushroom spring roll, subtly spiced with ginger, lemon zest, garlic, and green Thai chiles. It is eaten wrapped in tender leaves of Boston lettuce and dipped in a piquant dipping sauce.

"I was inspired by a food hawker," Mr. Vongerichten said. "It was a woman who ran a food stand that sold only vegetarian spring rolls. She had around twelve different kinds of spring rolls, and the mushroom roll really stood out. It was so flavorful and creamy. I tried to talk to her to find out what was in it, but she didn't speak English.

"So after tasting it, I did my best to figure out the ingredients, and the recipe we use at Spice Market is what we came up with. I think it's pretty close to what we had on the street that day."

1. For the dipping sauce: In a small bowl, combine the sambal oelek, honey, lemon juice, rice wine vinegar, and salt. Mix well. Cover and refrigerate for up to 1 week.

2. For the mushroom filling: Combine the butter and garlic in a sauté pan over medium-high heat, and stir until the butter is foamy and garlic is fragrant but not browned. Add the oyster mushrooms, shiitake mushrooms, chile, and salt to taste. Cover and cook over medium heat until the mushrooms have released their juices and are soft and glazed, about 6 minutes. Add the lemon zest, ginger, and chervil

{continued}

1½ tablespoons finely grated (preferably on a Microplane grater) lemon zest

1 tablespoon finely grated (preferably on a Microplane grater) peeled ginger

1 tablespoon chopped fresh chervil or 1 teaspoon chopped fresh tarragon

8 spring roll wrappers

1 large egg yolk, beaten

3 cups vegetable oil, or as needed

Ground white pepper (optional)

8 Boston lettuce leaves

or tarragon, and sauté 1 minute. Remove from the heat and spread across a small pan. Place in the freezer, uncovered, mixing occasionally until very cold, about 15 minutes.

3. Place a spring roll wrapper in front of you, like a diamond, so a point faces you. Lightly brush the four corners of the wrapper with the beaten egg yolk. Place 2 tablespoons mushroom mixture into the bottom quarter of the wrapper. Starting from the bottom corner, roll the wrapper twice. Fold the side corners toward the middle, and continue rolling until closed. Repeat to make 8 spring rolls.

4. In a deep fryer, wok, or skillet, heat the oil to 350°F. Add the spring rolls, working in batches if necessary, and fry until golden brown, about 5 minutes. Remove with a slotted spoon. Drain on paper towels. If desired, season lightly with salt and white pepper. Place 2 lettuce leaves on each of four plates and arrange a spring roll on each leaf. Divide the dipping sauce among four very small bowls and place a bowl on each plate.

Mushroom Quesadillas

Adapted from Rosa Mexicano restaurants

TIME: *40 minutes*
YIELD: *3 servings (six 6-inch quesadillas or three 10-inch quesadillas)*

12 ounces mixed mushrooms (such as cremini, portobello, shiitake, oyster), trimmed and thinly sliced

3/4 cup finely chopped white onion

3 garlic cloves, finely chopped

2 serrano chiles, trimmed, seeded, cored, and finely chopped

3 tablespoons extra-virgin olive oil

Salt

4 ounces queso chihuahua, Monterey Jack, Muenster, or Cheddar cheese, finely shredded (to make 1½ cups, loosely packed)

Joseph Quintana, the executive chef of Rosa Mexicano Lincoln Center, is Puerto Rican, born in Brooklyn and a graduate of the New York Restaurant School.

So how did he become a chef specializing in Mexican food?

He had a mentor—his brother-in-law Jose Huerta, a sous-chef at P. J. Clarke's. "At family meals, he taught me how to cook Mexican food," Mr. Quintana said.

Mr. Quintana has also visited Mexico several times with the Rosa Mexicano management. "In Mexico, on every single corner, there are trucks selling quesadillas—some grilled, some fried," he said.

Rosa Mexicano restaurants serve *quesadillas con huitlacoche* (quesadillas with corn fungus), but here Mr. Quintana has adapted the recipe for mushrooms, which are much easier to find. He also suggests adding epazote leaves as an option. "The epazote has a sharp taste, a little like a sharp anise."

The recipe consists of a sauté of mushrooms and a sprinkle of salt, then filling the quesadillas with the mushrooms, cheese, and epazote and turning them in the griddle until the cheese melts and the tortillas are crisp and golden.

It's a delectable no-brainer.

1. In a medium bowl, mix the mushrooms, onion, garlic, and chiles until well combined.

{continued}

Six 6-inch (or three 10-inch)
  fresh corn tortillas
6 fresh epazote leaves
  (optional)
Sour cream, for serving
Salsa verde, for serving

2. Place the oil in a large heavy skillet over medium-high heat and heat until the oil is shimmering. Add the mushroom mixture, season very lightly with salt, and cook, stirring and tossing, until the mushrooms are browned, 6 to 10 minutes. Scrape into a bowl and season with more salt if needed.

3. Divide the cheese among the tortillas, spreading a portion over half of each tortilla, leaving a small empty border, about 1 inch, at the edge. Divide the mushroom mixture among the tortillas, placing it on top of the cheese. Divide the epazote leaves, if using, among the tortillas. Fold the empty side over the filling and press firmly to close.

4. Heat a cast-iron or other heavy griddle over medium heat. Cook the quesadillas in batches, turning once, until light golden brown and crisp, about 3 minutes per side. Serve immediately, with sour cream and salsa verde on the side.

Roasted Mushrooms with Garlic

*Adapted from Josh Blakely,
Executive Chef, Macao Trading Company*

TIME: *45 minutes*
YIELD: *2 appetizer servings
or 2 side servings*

4 cups mixed mushrooms
(such as shiitake, morel,
oyster, and chanterelle), cut
into 1-inch pieces

2/3 cup extra-virgin olive oil

8 whole garlic cloves

4–5 sprigs of thyme

Salt and freshly ground black
pepper

4 garlic cloves, finely grated
(on a Microplane or cheese
grater)

Half a dried red chile or 1/2
teaspoon crushed red
pepper flakes

2 tablespoons sherry vinegar

1 plum tomato, seeded
and diced

2 tablespoons chopped
parsley

Josh Blakely, the executive chef at Macao Trading Company in TriBeCa in Manhattan, is from the Outer Banks of North Carolina, and his favorite foods are Spanish and Portuguese. "It's an uncanny resemblance to the food from the Outer Banks," he said. "It's the vinegar, the pork, the seafood, the oysters."

Two of his mentors are Eder Montero and Alexandra Raij, the husband-and-wife chefs and partners of Txikito, a Basque restaurant in Chelsea. Mr. Blakely's mushrooms with garlic is a dish for those who adore garlic. The mushrooms are roasted with whole cloves of garlic, and then sauced with a hot, bubbling vinaigrette dense with sautéed, golden bits of garlic. As a garnish, he adds chopped nuts.

"It's a distillation of all the al ajillo dishes I have eaten," Mr. Blakely said, referring to the garlic dishes of Spain, which include shrimp in a piping hot garlic sauce. He has been to Portugal once, to Spain twice, and spent years at Tia Pol, also in Chelsea, where Mr. Montero and Ms. Raij were chefs and partners. When he cooks delicate mushrooms like oysters, chanterelles, or hen of the woods, he said, "My favorite thing to do with the little guys is to roast them in a pan, and not touch them very much, and let the flavor develop."

1. Preheat the oven to 400°F. In a shallow roasting pan, mix together the mushrooms, 1/3 cup of the olive oil, the whole garlic gloves, and the thyme. Season with salt and pepper to taste. Roast, stirring

{continued}

1 teaspoon pimenton
    (smoked Spanish paprika)
2 tablespoons chopped
    roasted, salted Marcona
    almonds, cashews, or
    peanuts

occasionally, until the mushrooms are golden brown and just starting to crisp, about 30 minutes. Remove from the oven, and discard the thyme and garlic. Arrange the mushrooms in a shallow bowl, 6 to 8 inches in diameter.

2. In a small sauté pan, heat the remaining ⅓ cup olive oil until shimmering. Add the grated garlic and chile. Sauté until golden brown, and immediately add the vinegar, the tomato, 1 tablespoon of the parsley, and a pinch of salt. Remove from the heat and immediately pour over the mushrooms.

3. Garnish with the remaining 1 tablespoon chopped parsley, the pimenton, and the chopped almonds. Serve immediately, while bubbly and hot. If desired, serve with grilled, crusty bread.

Roasted Mushrooms with Goat Cheese and Grits

Adapted from Brian Ellis, Executive Chef, Jane

TIME: *45 minutes*
YIELD: *6 servings*

FOR THE MUSHROOMS:

1 cup shiitake mushrooms, cleaned and hard stems discarded

1 cup oyster mushrooms, cleaned and hard stems discarded

1 cup cremini mushrooms, cleaned and hard stems discarded

¼ cup extra-virgin olive oil

1 sprig thyme

4 garlic cloves

Salt and freshly ground black pepper

The unusual marriage of ingredients in this dish served at Jane is described by Brian Ellis, the restaurant's executive chef, as "a Southern twist on the Italian dish of roast mushrooms and polenta."

Whatever its cultural origins, the combination of roasted mushrooms and grits is pure comfort food, with a slight touch of sophistication. The jalapeño pepper perks it up and the goat cheese enriches it.

Ellis points out that oyster mushrooms are delicate—if they sit around after being roasted, "They can dry up," he said. "So if you're not going to eat them right away, don't cook them until just before serving." You should do a quick eight-minute sauté and add them to the roasted mushrooms.

He introduced the dish in the spring, but it is a year-round, multi-purpose dish: "You can have it for breakfast, lunch, dinner, or late night."

1. For the mushrooms: Preheat the oven to 400°F. In a mixing bowl, combine the shiitakes, oyster mushrooms, creminis, olive oil, thyme, and garlic. Season with salt and pepper to taste. Transfer to a sheet pan and roast for 15 minutes. Remove from the oven, discard the thyme and garlic, and cover to keep warm. While the mushrooms are roasting, prepare the grits.

{continued}

FOR THE GRITS:

2 cups milk

1 jalapeño pepper, split
  and seeded

1 garlic clove

1 bay leaf

1 sprig rosemary

1 teaspoon kosher salt

1 cup organic grits

2 tablespoons butter

2 ounces fresh goat cheese

2. For the grits: In a saucepan over medium heat, combine the milk, 2 cups water, jalapeño, garlic, bay leaf, rosemary, and salt. Bring to a simmer, then remove from the heat. Pour through a fine-mesh strainer into a heatproof bowl and discard the solids.

3. Return the liquid to the saucepan and place over high heat to bring to a boil. Add the grits, lower the heat to medium, and stir constantly until fully cooked and smooth, 15 to 20 minutes. Add the butter and mix well.

4. Add the goat cheese immediately before serving and mix well. Divide the grits among six plates and spoon the roasted mushrooms over the grits.

N

for Noodles and Pastas

Basil, Spinach, and Arugula Pesto

Adapted from Vincent Chirico, Executive Chef-Owner, Vai

TIME: *1 hour*
YIELD: *2 servings*

FOR THE GARLIC CONFIT:

³/₄ cup olive oil, or as needed

10 garlic cloves

FOR THE PESTO:

4 ounces basil or chervil

2 ounces baby spinach

2 ounces baby arugula

¹/₄ cup hazelnuts, toasted
    and finely ground

¹/₄ cup grated ricotta salata

Salt and freshly ground
    black pepper

Cooked linguine or other
    pasta, for serving (optional)

Many people make pesto from fresh basil, pine nuts, garlic, olive oil, cheeses, and butter. The basil is raw, as is the garlic.

The result? Pungent and delicious.

At Vai in Manhattan, Vincent Chirico, the executive chef and owner, briefly blanches the essential greens—basil or chervil, spinach, and arugula—until they become bright green and tender. He then plunges the vegetables into an ice bath, drains and squeezes them dry, and then blends them with garlic confit, hazelnuts, and ricotta salata.

The result? Less pungent, but still delicious.

Asked why he makes a cooked, rather than raw, pesto, he said, "I prefer it cooked. It seems more palatable, it keeps its color better, it emulsifies better, it coats the pasta a little bit better." The swift blanching of the vegetables barely diminishes the freshness, he said, and by simmering the garlic in olive oil, the garlic confit adds both a mellowness and creaminess.

At Vai, Mr. Chirico uses chervil, rather than basil, because he always has a lot of it on hand. Chervil, however, is not easy to find at supermarkets, or even at greenmarkets, so he suggests substituting basil, which is much more available.

1. For the garlic confit: Heat ¹/₂ cup olive oil in a small pan over low heat until warm. Add the garlic cloves and cook until very soft, about

{continued}

30 minutes. Using a slotted spoon, remove the garlic cloves, reserving both the cloves and the oil.

2. For the pesto: Have a large bowl of ice water ready. In a small pot over high heat, bring 4 cups water to a boil and blanch the basil or chervil until tender, about 30 seconds. Remove with a slotted spoon and transfer to ice water. Place the spinach and arugula in boiling water until bright green and tender, about a minute. Drain well and transfer to the ice water. When the greens are well chilled, drain well, place in a kitchen towel, and squeeze as hard as possible to remove the excess moisture.

3. In a blender, combine half the garlic cloves, half the garlic cooking oil, half the blanched greens (basil or chervil, spinach, and arugula), half the hazelnuts, and half the ricotta salata. Blend 5 minutes.

4. Add the remaining garlic cloves, garlic cooking oil, blanched greens, hazelnuts, and ricotta salata. Blend, adding ¼ cup additional olive oil, or more as needed, for 2 to 5 minutes, to make a thick but pourable pesto. Season with salt and pepper to taste. Blend 1 minute more. If desired, serve over hot linguine or other pasta.

Cold Noodles with Peanut Sauce (Vegan)

Adapted from Elaine Louie and Julia Chang Bloch

TIME: *25 minutes*
YIELD: *2 to 3 servings*

6 ounces Chinese noodles

1½ cups peeled, seeded, julienned cucumber

1 teaspoon salt

¼ cup creamy peanut butter

1 tablespoon soy sauce

2 tablespoons balsamic or Chinese black vinegar

2 teaspoons sugar

1 tablespoon sesame oil

1 teaspoon rice wine or dry sherry

1 teaspoon hot bean paste

1 teaspoon hot chili oil

1 teaspoon minced peeled fresh ginger

3 garlic cloves, minced

1 scallion, trimmed and minced

1 cup bean sprouts

2 tablespoons roasted salted Chinese or other peanuts, coarsely chopped or crushed

In the early '80s, when Julia Chang Bloch and I created this version of a Chinese classic, we wanted to make it sprightly, vivid, and crunchy. What gives it texture are the cucumbers, bean sprouts, and especially the roasted, salted peanuts.

1. Bring a medium pan of water to a boil, add the noodles, and cook until tender, 3 to 5 minutes. Drain into a colander, rinse under cold water, and shake to remove the excess water. Set aside to cool.

2. In a small bowl, combine the cucumber and salt. Mix well and set aside.

3. In a medium bowl, combine the peanut butter and 2 tablespoons hot water; whisk until smooth. Add the soy sauce, vinegar, sugar, sesame oil, rice wine or dry sherry, hot bean paste, hot chili oil, ginger, garlic, and scallion. Whisk until smooth. Add the noodles to the bowl and mix with the sauce.

4. Drain the cucumbers, wrap in a towel, and squeeze firmly to remove the excess moisture. Garnish the noodles with the cucumbers and bean sprouts. Sprinkle with the crushed peanuts and serve.

Fregola

Adapted from Lee McGrath, Executive Chef, Po

TIME: *30 minutes*
YIELD: *2 servings*

Salt

8 ounces fregola (available in specialty food stores)

1 tablespoon butter

1½ cups fresh sweet corn kernels or frozen peas or asparagus, peeled, trimmed, and cut into slices ¼ inch thick

1 cup sliced scallions

1 cup hot vegetable stock

3 tablespoons grated Parmigiano-Reggiano or grana padano cheese, or as needed

Freshly ground black pepper

Green salad, for serving (optional)

Fregola are tiny toothsome balls of pasta that marry happily with fresh corn, peas, or asparagus. "Just keep everything small," said Lee McGrath, the executive chef at Po in Manhattan. The end result is "kind of like macaroni and cheese," he said. The pasta is cooked. The vegetables, along with scallions, simmer, in a lively fashion, for a few minutes, and the two—pasta and vegetables—are tossed together with a handful of Parmigiano-Reggiano.

The recipe is simplicity itself, and the time, from the mincing of the scallions to the final finished dish, is only 30 minutes.

1. In a medium pot, bring lightly salted water to a boil. Add the fregola and cook until tender yet springy and chewy, 12 to 14 minutes.

2. Drain, rinse under cool water, and drain again. Set aside.

3. Place a sauté pan over medium-high heat, and add the butter, corn or peas or asparagus, scallions, and vegetable stock. Cook at a lively simmer, stirring occasionally, until the corn or peas or asparagus are cooked and the broth is reduced by about half, about 3 minutes.

4. Remove from the heat, and add the fregola and cheese. The mixture should be gooey like macaroni and cheese. Season with salt and pepper to taste and serve. If desired, serve with a green salad.

Korean Sweet Potato Noodles (*Jap Chae*) (Vegan)

Adapted from New Wonjo Restaurant

TIME: 1 hour, plus 1 to 2 hours'
soaking of dried mushrooms,
if using
YIELD: 2 servings

4 ounces Korean dried sweet
potato noodles

3 teaspoons sesame oil

2 tablespoons soy sauce

2 teaspoons sugar

2 tablespoons peanut or other
vegetable oil

2 napa or other cabbage
leaves, thinly sliced

Half a carrot, julienned (to
make about 1/4 cup)

Half a small onion, thinly sliced
(to make about 1/4 cup)

1/4 teaspoon minced garlic

3 scallions, white and light
green parts only, trimmed
and cut into 2-inch lengths

If ever there was a dish meant for nimble, quick eating (forget languorous flirtation over dinner) it's this, the Korean *Jap Chae,* a shiny tangle of translucent sweet potato noodles with sliced mushrooms, cabbage, carrots, onions, and spinach. "It should be eaten quickly or, after 30 minutes, the noodles will begin to stick together," said Christina Jang, an owner of New Wonjo Restaurant in Manhattan. (To reheat it, she suggests adding a half tablespoon of sesame oil.)

"People eat noodles for longevity," Ms. Jang added. "So it is served at birthdays, but also family gatherings, or any big party."

It is a dish with lovely textures, the slippery noodles, the silken mushrooms, and the crunchy carrots and cabbage. The seasoning is a light-handed mix of garlic, soy sauce, sugar, and sesame oil, and a final sprinkle of toasted sesame seeds.

Jap Chae also lends itself to using whatever is on hand. "You can use carrots or sliced sweet red bell pepper for color, and you can use any kind of mushrooms," Ms. Jang said.

1. Bring a medium pot of water to a boil. Add the noodles and cook until tender-chewy, about 5 minutes. Drain and rinse with cold water. Shake the excess water off and transfer to a bowl. Using kitchen shears, cut the noodles into 8-inch lengths. Add 1 1/2 teaspoons sesame oil, mix well, and set aside.

{continued}

4 fresh or dried shiitake
mushrooms that have been
soaked 1 to 2 hours,
stemmed and thinly sliced
10 spinach leaves and stems,
washed well, drained, and
squeezed dry
1/4 teaspoon freshly ground
black pepper
1 teaspoon toasted sesame
seeds

2. In a small bowl, combine the soy sauce and sugar. Mix well and set aside.

3. Place a wok or large sauté pan over high heat, add the peanut oil, and swirl to coat the entire wok or pan. When the oil is shimmering, add the cabbage, carrot, and onion, and cook until tender, stirring occasionally, 1 to 3 minutes.

4. Add the garlic, scallions, and mushrooms. Fry until the scallions begin to soften, about 1 minute. Add the spinach, soy sauce–sugar mixture, noodles, and black pepper. Cook until the noodles are heated through, stirring vigorously, about 3 minutes. Turn off the heat, and add the sesame seeds and remaining 1 1/2 teaspoons sesame oil. Mix well. Divide between two plates and serve.

Mac & Cheese

Adapted from Maximo Lopez May, Executive Chef, Wall & Water

TIME: *1 hour and 30 minutes*
YIELD: *4 servings*

Sea salt

1 pound dry strascinati, strozzapreti, orecchiette, cavatelli, or rigatoni pasta

4 tablespoons unsalted butter, plus 1 tablespoon for buttering the baking dish

4 slices day-old country bread, cut into ¾-inch cubes

2 tablespoons minced fresh thyme leaves

1 small onion, finely chopped

2 garlic cloves

4 cups oyster mushrooms, trumpet mushrooms, or hen of the woods, wiped clean, trimmed, and left whole, if small, or cut lengthwise, in half or thirds, if large

Can mac and cheese be haute?

Yes, in the hands of Maximo Lopez May, the executive chef of Wall & Water at the Andaz Wall Street Hotel in Manhattan, who adds exotic mushrooms to the dish. "It only works if the mushrooms are great, so it is ideal to make it during the fall season, when mushrooms are best. Go for elegant ones, like chanterelles or trumpets." If your budget doesn't allow for the pricey ones, then use oyster mushrooms, trumpet mushrooms, hen of the woods, or cremini. But use a mix.

The cheese can be Cato Corner Bloomsday cheese, Gruyère, or Emmental, and the wine used in the reduction should be whatever you plan to drink during dinner.

The final mac and cheese?

It will be gooey, rich, and luxe.

1. Preheat the oven to 350°F. Bring a large pot of lightly salted water to a boil. Add the pasta and cook until al dente, 10 to 13 minutes, depending on the size of the pasta. Drain and set aside.

2. In a small pan over medium heat, melt 4 tablespoons butter. Remove from the heat and set aside. In a small bowl, combine the bread, thyme, and half the melted butter. Mix and set aside.

{continued}

2 tablespoons extra-virgin
    olive oil (optional)
1 cup white wine
1 cup heavy cream
1 cup milk, or as needed
10 ounces, or as needed, Cato
    Corner Bloomsday, Gruyère,
    or Emmental cheese,
    grated or finely chopped
Finely grated zest of 2 lemons
1/4 cup roughly chopped fresh
    parsley leaves
Freshly ground black pepper

3. In a large sauté pan over medium heat, combine the remaining melted butter, onion, and garlic. Sauté until the onion is translucent, 3 to 5 minutes. Add the mushrooms, adding olive oil if the pan looks dry, and sauté until tender, about 12 minutes.

4. When the mushrooms are tender, add the wine and stir until it has evaporated. Add the cream and 1 cup milk, and bring to a boil. Add the pasta, 10 ounces grated cheese, lemon zest, and chopped parsley. Mix well, and season with salt and pepper to taste. If desired, add more milk and cheese as needed for a creamy, cheesy sauce.

5. Butter a 10-inch-diameter by 3- to 4-inch-deep baking dish. Pour in the pasta mixture, and top with the bread mixture. Bake, uncovered, until the bread turns golden brown, 7 to 10 minutes. Serve hot.

Mushroom and Chive Panfried Noodles (Vegan)

Adapted from Yvonne Wong

TIME: 1 hour
YIELD: 2 servings

8 ounces dried thin wheat or
egg Chinese or Japanese
noodles

2 tablespoons plus 1 cup
vegetable oil

2 tablespoons julienned fresh
ginger

2 cups yellow and/or green
chives, trimmed, cut
crosswise into 2-inch pieces

1 cup Prince mushrooms,
trimmed, sliced diagonally
¼ inch thick, and then
sliced into ¼-inch-wide
strips

1 cup oyster mushrooms,
trimmed and halved or
quartered lengthwise

1 cup baby portobello or baby
shiitake or cremini, stemmed
and halved or quartered

Yvonne Wong, an excellent home cook, a former Chinese antiques dealer, and a former restaurateur (The Ultimate Lotus in midtown Manhattan), has a current food obsession.

"Have I told you about the Prince mushroom?" she asked, eyes twinkling. "It has the texture of abalone, but not the price." The fresh mushrooms sell for $2 a pound, and fresh abalone sells for $60 to $80 a pound. (Dried abalone sells for $99 to $550 a pound.)

On a late October day, she threaded her way through the crowds at Hong Kong Market in Manhattan's Chinatown, and picked out some Prince mushrooms, among other things. She had not told me what the Prince mushroom looks like.

It resembles an erect male organ.

She suggested sautéing the mushrooms with ginger and chives, and binding it with a light sauce of vegetable broth, soy sauce, and vegetarian oyster sauce. The vegetables are put on top of panfried noodles, then garnished with a sprinkle of white pepper, sesame oil, julienned ginger, cilantro, and a drizzle of balsamic vinegar.

1. Bring a large pot of water to a boil over high heat. Add the noodles and cook according to package directions until tender. Drain under cold water into a colander. Drain again, vigorously shaking the colander to remove excess moisture. Allow the noodles to dry for at least 30 minutes, shaking occasionally; the drier the noodles, the better they will fry.

{continued}

1½ cups vegetable broth

2 tablespoons soy sauce

2 teaspoons vegetarian
   oyster sauce

1½ teaspoons cornstarch

Salt and white pepper

10 cilantro leaves, for garnish

2 teaspoons sesame oil

1 teaspoon vinegar

2. In a large skillet or wok over medium-high heat, heat 2 tablespoons oil until shimmering. Add 1 tablespoon ginger and stir rapidly for 30 seconds. Add the chives and stir for 30 seconds. Add the Prince, oyster, and portobello mushrooms, and stir-fry until softened, about 8 minutes. Transfer to a platter and set aside.

3. In a small bowl, mix the vegetable broth, soy sauce, and oyster sauce; set aside. In another small bowl, mix the cornstarch with 2 tablespoons cold water; set aside.

4. In a large skillet over high heat, heat the remaining 1 cup vegetable oil to 350°F. Add the noodles, shaping into a pancake, and fry until golden on one side, about 4 minutes. Turn over and fry until golden on the other side. Using a wide wire-mesh strainer, transfer the noodles to paper towels to drain. Discard the oil and return the pan to high heat.

5. Add the stock mixture and bring to a boil. Add the cornstarch mixture and stir for 20 seconds. Add the mushroom and chives mixture and heat through. Season with salt and white pepper to taste.

6. Transfer the noodles to a platter, and pour the mushroom and chives mixture over the noodles. Garnish with the remaining tablespoon of julienned ginger and cilantro leaves. Drizzle with the sesame oil, sprinkle with the vinegar, and serve.

NOTE: Choose thin dried Chinese or Japanese noodles, and be sure to read the back of the package to see if the noodles can be boiled and then fried. Some noodles can only be boiled and won't fry crisply.

Orzotto with Zucchini and Pesto

Adapted from Cesare Casella,
Executive Chef and a Partner, Salumeria Rosi

TIME: 45 minutes
YIELD: 4 servings

FOR THE PESTO:

1 tablespoon pine nuts
(optional)

½ garlic clove, finely chopped

½ cup firmly packed
basil leaves

3 tablespoons extra-virgin
olive oil

1 tablespoon grated
Parmigiano-Reggiano cheese

2 teaspoons grated Pecorino
Romano cheese

Salt and freshly ground
black pepper

Chile flakes

An orzotto is like a risotto except that orzo, the rice-shaped pasta, is used instead of rice. And why might you want to do that?

"Orzo is easier to work with than rice, because the rice is much more delicate and easy to overcook," said Cesare Casella, the executive chef and a partner at Salumeria Rosi on the Upper West Side of Manhattan.

"With the rice, you have only 12 to 16 minutes to cook it, and then it becomes overcooked," he said. "For orzo, you need 20 to 40 minutes, depending on the orzo. You can also cook it three-quarters of the way and hold it, chilled, in the refrigerator and add the last half cup of broth and half cup of water the next day." With orzo, he said, "You have more flexibility."

"In Italy, you use risotto with every kind of vegetable," he added. At the Union Square Greenmarket, he particularly liked the zucchini: "Sometimes zucchini are bitter and watery. But this year, they're good," firm and sweet. Mr. Casella said he will serve orzotto at Salumeria Rosi "until the end of the good zucchini."

The finished dish is creamy and pale gold in color. The pesto nearly dissolves into the orzotto for a subtly nuanced flavor, and surprisingly there is barely a hint of green, except for the lightly browned zucchini.

{continued}

FOR THE ORZOTTO:

2 cups vegetable broth

3 tablespoons olive oil

1/3 cup chopped white onion

1 cup orzo

1/2 cup white wine

Salt

1/3 cup (generous) diced
   zucchini

1/3 cup grated Parmigiano-
   Reggiano cheese

1. For the pesto: In a small food processor or blender, combine the pine nuts (if using), garlic, and basil. Pulse to chop, then while continuing to pulse, slowly pour in the oil to make a chunky mixture; do not puree. Transfer to a small bowl, and add the tablespoon of Parmigiano-Reggiano and the Pecorino Romano. Mix well, and season with salt, pepper, and chile flakes to taste. Set aside.

2. For the orzotto: Place the vegetable broth in a small saucepan and bring to a bare simmer. In another small saucepan, bring 2 cups lightly salted water to a bare simmer. In a skillet over medium heat, combine 2 tablespoons olive oil and the onion, and sauté until soft and translucent, 5 to 10 minutes. Add the orzo and sauté until lightly toasted, 1 to 2 minutes. Add the wine and sauté until evaporated. Season lightly with salt.

3. Add 1 cup hot broth and simmer, stirring constantly, until the liquid is almost absorbed. Add 1 cup hot water and repeat. Continue to alternately add broth and water 1/2 cup at a time until the orzotto is tender; the total cooking time will be 16 to 20 minutes and all the broth or water may not be needed. The finished orzo should be golden yellow (add too much water and the flavor will be weak; add too much broth and the color will darken). Set aside the finished orzo, cover, and keep warm.

4. In a small skillet over medium heat, heat the remaining 1 tablespoon olive oil and add the zucchini. Sauté until lightly browned, about 5 minutes. Stir the zucchini and 2 tablespoons pesto into the orzo (reserve any remaining pesto for another use). Add the 1/3 cup Parmigiano-Reggiano, stir until melted, and adjust the salt as needed. Serve immediately.

Pad Thai

Adapted from Bruce Cost, Chef and Cookbook Author

TIME: *45 minutes*
YIELD: *2 servings*

5⅓ ounces dried pad thai rice
   noodles (see Note)
2 tablespoons freshly
   squeezed lime juice and
   2 lime wedges, for garnish
1 tablespoon light brown sugar
½ teaspoon ground red Thai
   bird chiles or cayenne
   pepper
½ teaspoon paprika
2 tablespoons Thai sweet
   chili sauce
2 tablespoons soy sauce
1 cup peanut oil
8 green beans, trimmed
1 large egg
¼ cup finely diced red onion
2 baby bok choy, quartered
   lengthwise

Pad thai, savory noodles that are a national dish of Thailand, can be made in multiple variations, but cooks must stay on their toes.

At its sprightly best, pad thai has fresh, tangy flavors. The sauce—with a splash of lime or lemon juice—is sweet, sour, and spicy. The gently chewy, translucent rice noodles are mixed with a toss of bean sprouts, baby bok choy, slivers of sweet red pepper, string beans, and a sprinkle of fresh basil and cilantro. Tiny clouds of scrambled egg and cubes of swiftly sautéed tofu add protein. The final touch is a topping of chopped roasted salted peanuts.

At its worst, when the dish has been left on the burner too long, "The balance goes off, the sugar burns off, the noodles get soggy and it can have a big, salty, sour taste, or it can taste scorched or caramelized," Bruce Cost said.

Mr. Cost is a partner in the eight Big Bowl restaurants in Illinois, Minnesota, and Virginia, and the author of several cookbooks, including *Big Bowl Noodles and Rice*.

How does he teach his cooks, none of them Thai, to make the dish perfectly? He runs drills, showing them that the moment they add the lime mixture to the dish, they must take it off the heat, add the scrambled egg, basil, cilantro, and bean sprouts and serve it immediately.

"The clean, bright taste is delicate," he said. "If it sits there for an extra minute or two, it's ruined."

{continued}

1/4 large red bell pepper,
  cut into julienne
1 cup lightly packed thinly
  sliced napa cabbage
2 scallions, halved crosswise
  and quartered lengthwise
1/2 cup finely diced firm tofu
1/4 cup plus 1 tablespoon pad
  thai sauce (see Note)
1/4 cup mixed chopped fresh
  basil and cilantro leaves
1/2 to 3/4 cup fresh bean
  sprouts
2 to 4 tablespoons coarsely
  chopped roasted salted
  peanuts

1. Place the noodles in a bowl and cover with very hot tap water. Allow to sit for 30 minutes. Meanwhile, in a small bowl, combine the lime juice, brown sugar, ground chiles, paprika, Thai sweet chili sauce, and soy sauce; reserve. Drain the noodles well, rinse with cold water, and set aside.

2. Place the oil in a wok over medium-high heat and heat to 325°F. Add the green beans and fry until wrinkled, about 1 1/2 minutes. Transfer the beans to a plate and discard all but 3 tablespoons oil. Return to medium-high heat and add the egg, stirring quickly to set it and scramble it slightly. Transfer to a plate and set aside.

3. To the wok add the red onion, bok choy, red bell pepper, napa cabbage, and scallions, tossing for 1 to 2 minutes. Add the noodles and toss until coated with oil and almost softened. Add the tofu, wrinkled beans, and pad thai sauce; toss until thoroughly heated.

4. Drizzle in the reserved lime juice mixture and toss for 5 seconds. Remove the pan from the heat immediately, then add the scrambled egg, basil and cilantro mixture, and bean sprouts. Transfer to a heated serving platter, and garnish with peanuts and lime wedges. Serve immediately.

NOTE: Pad thai noodles and sauce are sold in Asian markets and online.

Stir-Fried Glass Noodles, Malaysian Hawker Style

Adapted from Simpson Wong, Executive Chef-Owner, Café Asean

TIME: 50 minutes
YIELD: 1 large serving

FOR THE NOODLES:

3 ounces dried glass noodles

FOR THE COOKING SAUCE:

2 tablespoons tamarind paste

2 teaspoons soy sauce

1 teaspoon Indonesian
   sweet soy sauce,
   preferably ABC brand

1 teaspoon oyster sauce
   (optional)

1 teaspoon sesame oil

1/2 teaspoon hot chili paste

FOR THE GARNISH SAUCE:

2 tablespoons Thai sweet
   chili sauce

1 tablespoon fresh lime juice

1/2 fresh Thai bird chile pepper,
   seeded and minced

1 garlic clove, minced

Simpson Wong, the owner and executive chef of Café Asean in Greenwich Village, grew up in Tanjung Malim, Malaysia, a small town of seventy houses, where the local school did not serve lunch. "You walked home to eat lunch," he said. By the time he was ten, he had graduated to buying lunch from a food cart. "Between classes, you ate on the street," said Mr. Wong, who is Malaysian Chinese. Street hawkers would sell the students piping-hot stir-fried glass noodles with seafood, served on a banana leaf, for 10 cents.

A vegetarian version of this dish was prepared by monks at the local Buddhist temples and provided free to worshippers. It is a light and quick-cooking dish. The carrots, chives, string beans, and bean sprouts are crunchy, and the sauce is piquant. "You have the balance of sweetness from the sweet soy sauce, sourness from the tamarind, and spice from the chile paste," Mr. Wong said. The final garnish is a dollop of a second, equally perky concoction—Thai sweet chili sauce mixed with fresh lime juice, minced fresh Thai bird chile, and minced garlic.

1. For the noodles: Soak the dried glass noodles in 4 cups warm water for 30 minutes. Drain and set aside. While the noodles are soaking, prepare the cooking sauce and the garnish sauce.

2. For the cooking sauce: In a small bowl, mix the tamarind paste with 3 tablespoons water. Using a metal spoon or your fingers, break

{continued}

3 tablespoons canola or
  other vegetable oil

1 large egg

2 garlic cloves, minced

1/2 cup julienned carrot, in
  1 1/2-inch lengths

1/2 cup Chinese garlic chives
  or other chives, in 1 1/2-inch
  lengths

1/2 cup trimmed julienned
  green beans, in 1 1/2-inch
  lengths

1 cup bean sprouts

1/2 lime, cut into wedges

the tamarind into small pieces to infuse the water. Allow to sit for a few minutes. Place a small strainer over a clean bowl and strain the tamarind mixture, squeezing it to remove all the liquid; discard the solids. There will be 1 to 1 1/2 tablespoons of a slightly thick liquid. Add the soy sauce, sweet soy sauce, oyster sauce (if using), sesame oil, and hot chili paste. Mix well and set aside.

3. For the garnish sauce: In a small bowl, mix together the Thai sweet chili sauce, lime juice, minced fresh Thai bird chile, and garlic. Set aside.

4. To finish and serve: Place a wok or large sauté pan over medium-high heat. Add 2 tablespoons canola oil and heat until shimmering. Add the egg, and when the bottom and edge are starting to form a crust, flip it and stir-fry until golden and almost crisp, breaking into rough strands. Add the remaining 1 tablespoon oil. Add the garlic and cook until fragrant but not brown, about 30 seconds. Add the carrot, chives, and green beans, and stir-fry until crisp-tender, 1 to 2 minutes. Add the noodles and continue to stir vigorously to keep the noodles from sticking, about 2 minutes. Add the cooking sauce and bean sprouts; toss well and stir-fry for 1 to 2 minutes. Drizzle the garnish sauce on top of the noodles as desired, and serve with lime wedges on the side.

Vietnamese Noodle Salad (Vegan)

Adapted from Michael Bao Huynh,
Executive Chef-Owner, DOB 111

TIME: *1 hour*
YIELD: *4 small appetizer servings,*
or 2 generous servings

FOR THE DRESSING:

1/4 cup sugar

1/3 cup soy sauce

1/2 cup fresh lime juice

1 garlic clove, minced

2 red Thai bird chiles,
seeded and minced

FOR THE SALAD:

6 ounces rice vermicelli
noodles

1/2 cup vegetable oil

1 pound firm tofu

2 garlic cloves, minced

1 cup baby bok choy or napa
cabbage, chopped into
1 1/2 by 1/2-inch pieces

On the last warm days of the year, Michael Bao Huynh, the executive chef and owner of DOB 111 in Manhattan, will make a crunchy yet slippery Vietnamese vegetarian noodle salad. It has both hot (as in cooked) and cold (as in raw) vegetables, a scattering of fresh herbs, and a piquant dressing made with fresh lime juice, garlic, Thai bird chiles, sugar, and soy sauce.

Mr. Huynh is from Saigon. He moved to the United States from Vietnam in 1982. He remembers his mother, Nghia Nguyen, making the noodle salad in Saigon for the local Buddhist temple on the day of the full moon celebration. "It's very light," he said.

Although the dish is not on the menu at DOB 111, he will make it on request.

1. For the dressing: In a bowl, combine the sugar, soy sauce, lime juice, and 3 tablespoons water. Whisk until the sugar is dissolved. Add the garlic and chiles and let stand for 1 hour before serving.

2. For the salad: Bring a medium-sized pot of water to a boil. Turn off the heat. Add the noodles to the water and soak until soft, 5 to 8 minutes. Drain, rinsing under cold water, and drain again. Using scissors, cut the noodles into 6-inch lengths. Set aside.

{continued}

1 cup fresh shiitake mushrooms, stemmed and cut into slender strips

1 tablespoon chopped seeded red Thai bird chiles

2 cups mung bean sprouts

1/2 cup scallions, trimmed and cut into 1-inch lengths

1 tablespoon soy sauce

1 cup julienned peeled seedless cucumber

2 cups red leaf lettuce, cut into 3/4-inch strips

1 teaspoon sesame oil

1/4 cup minced fresh mint

1/4 cup minced cilantro, plus 8 cilantro sprigs, for garnish

1/4 cup minced Thai basil

1/3 cup chopped roasted peanuts, for garnish

3. In a wok over high heat, add the oil and heat to 350°F. Pat the tofu dry with paper towels. Add to the wok and fry until golden on both sides, about 3 minutes. Using a wire strainer or spatula, transfer the tofu to paper towels, reserving the oil. Turn off the heat. When the tofu is cool enough to handle, cut it into 1/2-inch dice. Set aside.

4. Discard all but 2 tablespoons of the oil in the wok and return to high heat. When the oil is shimmering, add the diced tofu, garlic, bok choy or napa cabbage, mushrooms, and chiles. Stir-fry until the mushrooms are tender, about 3 minutes. Add the mung bean sprouts, scallions, and soy sauce; stir-fry just until crisp-tender, 2 to 3 minutes. Add 1/2 cup of the cucumber and cook 30 seconds.

5. In a large bowl, combine the lettuce, sesame oil, mint, cilantro, basil, and cooked vegetables. Toss lightly to combine. Divide the noodles among four (or two) bowls and top with equal parts of salad. Garnish with the remaining cucumber, roasted peanuts, and cilantro sprigs. Pass the dressing separately, to be spooned over the salad.

Miso French Onion Soup

Adapted from John Schenk,
Executive Chef, Strip House restaurants

TIME: *1 hour*
YIELD: *4 servings*

¼ cup plus 1 tablespoon
   olive oil
2½ pounds large Spanish
   onions, peeled, halved, and
   thinly sliced (about 4 cups)
8 diagonal baguette slices,
   about ¼ inch thick
⅓ cup miso
1 tablespoon finely chopped
   fresh thyme (optional)
Salt and freshly ground
   black pepper
4 large slices Swiss cheese

John Schenk, the big, hearty, executive chef of the six Strip House steakhouses nationwide, is a carnivore. His wife, Eun Joo Lee, is a vegetarian.

As part of his job, he visits each of the six restaurants at least once a month, which is more complicated than it sounds, because they are in New York, New Jersey, Florida, Texas, and Nevada.

Before he leaves on trips, he likes to make food that his wife can eat when he is away. And one of the things he likes to make is a rich French onion soup that he first ate in Boca Raton, Florida. When he described it to her, she liked the sound of sweet, caramelized onions topped by melted, bubbling Swiss cheese on croutons. Could he make her a vegetarian version?

He started sautéing the onions until they turned soft and brown, looked around their kitchen, and saw a box of miso.

That was the secret ingredient.

He mixed the miso and some chopped fresh thyme into boiling water, added the onions, and let it simmer for a few minutes. He poured the soup into crocks, and topped it with toasted croutons and Swiss cheese. He put the crocks on a tray and placed it under the broiler until both the soup and the cheese bubbled.

In a blind tasting, it's likely that few people would notice the absence of beef broth.

{continued}

1. Preheat the oven to 325°F. Place a large sauté pan over medium-high heat for 1 minute. Add ¼ cup olive oil and heat until shimmering. Add the onions and cook, stirring constantly and adjusting the heat as needed, until the onions are soft and deep golden brown, 20 to 25 minutes. Remove the pan from the heat and allow the onions to cool in the pan.

2. Brush both sides of the bread slices with the remaining 1 tablespoon olive oil and place on a baking sheet. Bake, turning once, until just crisp, about 4 minutes a side. Remove from the oven and set aside.

3. Pour 3 cups water into a 2-quart saucepan, cover, and bring to a boil. Add the miso, thyme (if using), and cooked onions; mix well. Simmer and season with salt and pepper as needed.

4. Preheat a broiler. Place a large ovenproof serving bowl or four small ovenproof bowls on a broiling pan or small baking sheet. Pour the hot soup into the large bowl or divide among the small bowls. Place the croutons on top of the soup and top with the Swiss cheese slices. Place the pan holding the soup directly under the broiler until the cheese is melted and the soup is bubbling. Serve immediately.

P

Hearts of Palm Tartlets (*Empadinhas de Palmito*)

Adapted from Antonia Ferreira

TIME: 1 hour and 15 minutes
YIELD: Twenty 2-inch savory tartlets (about 5 appetizer servings)

FOR THE TART CRUSTS:

1¼ cups all-purpose flour

¼ cup vegetable oil

1½ large egg yolks

6 tablespoons butter, at room temperature

Twenty 2-inch-diameter tartlet pans

FOR THE FILLING:

4 tablespoons butter

⅓ cup finely minced onion

¼ cup all-purpose flour

1½ cups milk

1½ cups thinly sliced (¼-inch-thick) hearts of palm, rinsed and drained

Salt and freshly ground black pepper

1 tablespoon finely grated Parmesan cheese

When Angela Mariani, a novelist based in Rio de Janeiro, visits New York City, she often hosts a party at her pied-à-terre, hiring Antonia Ferreira, a Brazilian cook and caterer in Queens. To start each event, Ms. Ferreira offers a tray of *empadinhas de palmito,* tiny, two-inch-wide savory tartlets filled with hearts of palm in a béchamel sauce. The delicate, buttery crust crumbles on the first bite.

"I learned how to make them at eleven, because we had no money," said Ms. Ferreira, who was born in Salvador, Brazil. She mastered making the *empadinhas*—the Portuguese word for little pastries that are typically stuffed—by watching people do it. As she kneaded, she explained, "When the hands are clean, the dough is ready." Then she molded the dough inside each tartlet pan, using her thumb and two fingers. She estimates that she can make hundreds of dishes—Brazilian, German, and Italian. The *empadinhas*, however, are her calling card.

1. For the tartlet crusts: In a large mixing bowl, combine the flour, oil, egg yolks, and butter. Using a spoon or by hand, mix until the dough is no longer sticky. Take a nub of dough about the size of a large marble, place it in a tartlet pan, and press very thinly to cover the inside (thick enough to cover but not so thin that the pan shows through). Pinch off the dough for a clean edge; set aside. Repeat with the remaining dough to make 20 tartlet crusts.

{continued}

2. For the filling: In a saucepan over medium heat, combine the butter and onion, and sauté until the onion is translucent, about 5 minutes. In a small bowl, combine the flour with 1 cup milk and whisk until smooth and blended. Add to the saucepan and stir until beginning to thicken.

3. Add the remaining ½ cup milk, reduce the heat to medium-low, and continue stirring until thickened, about 5 minutes. Add the hearts of palm, and season with salt and pepper to taste. Reduce the heat to low and simmer gently for 3 more minutes. Remove from the heat and set aside.

4. Preheat the oven to 300°F. Divide the mixture among the crust-filled pans and sprinkle with the cheese. Place on a baking sheet and bake until the tops are lightly golden, about 30 to 40 minutes. Cool to room temperature. Turn each pan upside down: The tartlet should fall into your hands upside down and all in one piece. Turn right side up and serve.

Sugar Snap Pea Salad

Adapted from Dan Kluger, Executive Chef, ABC Kitchen

TIME: *1 hour*
YIELD: *4 servings*

FOR THE DRESSING (MAKES ABOUT 1 QUART):

½ cup plus 1 teaspoon
    Champagne vinegar

¼ cup fresh lime juice

1½ tablespoons Dijon mustard

1 tablespoon kosher salt

1 teaspoon freshly ground
    black pepper

1 cup grated Parmigiano-
    Reggiano cheese

1 cup sunflower oil

½ cup extra-virgin olive oil

FOR THE SALAD:

Salt

3 cups sugar snap peas,
    trimmed

12 green Belgian endive leaves

12 red (or green) Belgian
    endive leaves

When ABC Kitchen opened in 2010 at ABC Home in Manhattan, I asked the waiter which dish was the most delicious one on the menu.

The sugar snap pea salad, he said.

And it was.

It is a salad best eaten in the summer, when the peas are at their sweetest. In November, the peas are "woodier," said Dan Kluger, the executive chef of ABC Kitchen. Although he does not offer the salad in the winter, a November sugar snap pea can still be sweet and crunchy, and the salad still sprightly.

The dressing is key. "It's cheesy and acidic," Mr. Kluger said, and it contrasts beautifully with the slightly bitter endive and the sweet peas.

The recipe calls for a quart of dressing, more than is necessary for four servings. "If you make a smaller quantity of the dressing, it won't emulsify," Mr. Kluger said. "You will get a soupy, lumpy mess." The dressing holds for up to three days, and then the fresh lime juice will fade. "It won't have the same sharpness," said Mr. Kluger, who pointed out that the salad makes a good hors d'oeuvre. Just serve a tray of single endive leaves or spears, topped with slivers of sugar snap peas, and daubed with dressing and a sprinkle of cheese.

1. For the dressing: In a blender, combine the vinegar, lime juice, mustard, salt, pepper, and Parmigiano-Reggiano. Blend for 30 seconds. Add the sunflower and olive oils. Blend until emulsified, about

{continued}

¼ cup grated Parmigiano-
  Reggiano cheese
2 tablespoons finely
  chopped parsley
2 tablespoons finely
  chopped chives
2 tablespoons finely
  chopped chervil
2 tablespoons finely
  chopped tarragon
Freshly ground black pepper

30 seconds. Transfer to a container and set aside. May be stored, covered and refrigerated, for up to 3 days.

2. Fill a large bowl with ice water and set aside. Bring a medium pot of heavily salted water to a boil. Add the sugar snap peas and blanch until crisp-tender, 20 to 30 seconds. Drain and plunge into ice water. Drain again and cut into chiffonade.

3. For the salad: To make one salad, place one green endive leaf and one red endive leaf on a plate. Top with a small mound of the sugar snap peas, and drizzle with a little dressing and 1 teaspoon Parmigiano-Reggiano. Repeat two more times using smaller endive spears each time. Top with a sprinkling of parsley, chives, chervil, and tarragon, and drizzle a little more dressing around the plate. Finish with a sprinkling of black pepper. Repeat to make a total of 4 salads.

Sweet Pea Crostini with Whipped Ricotta and Fresh Mint

Adapted from Joseph Ogrodnek, Executive Chef, Anella

TIME: *20 minutes*
YIELD: *2 servings*

3/4 cup fresh ricotta cheese

1 1/2 tablespoons extra-virgin olive oil, plus additional for brushing on bread

Salt and freshly ground black pepper

1/2 tablespoon butter

1 tablespoon minced shallot

1 cup fresh or frozen shelled peas

1 tablespoon finely chopped fresh mint

Lemon juice

Four 1/2-inch-thick rustic Italian bread slices

1 ounce coarsely grated pecorino cheese

Joseph Ogrodnek, the executive chef at Anella in Brooklyn, makes his own ricotta. "We heat milk, add lemon juice, and mix it with a little olive oil," he said. He uses the rich, creamy cheese as the base of a crostini, and tops it with a simple mix of sweet peas cooked with shallots in olive oil and butter, making sure to gently mash some of the peas so they do not roll off the crostini onto your lap and onto the floor.

Like most chefs, Mr. Ogrodnek likes to use his own homemade cheese and seasonal peas, bought from Rooftop Farm, two blocks from his restaurants. For home cooks, however, he suggests whipping store-bought fresh ricotta in a blender with a little olive oil to make it creamy and spreadable. Frozen peas can be a substitute for fresh, making this a year-round dish. The bread should be a nice, coarsely textured country bread, cut thick and toasted.

He tops it with a sprinkle of salt, pepper, mint, and lemon juice to cut the richness of the ricotta and the sweetness of the peas.

The crostini is a charming variation of an open-faced cheese sandwich.

1. Preheat the oven to 400°F. In a blender or small food processor, combine the ricotta and 1 tablespoon olive oil. Season with salt and pepper to taste. Puree until smooth and spreadable. Transfer to a covered container and refrigerate until needed.

{continued}

2. In a sauté pan over medium heat, melt the butter with ½ tablespoon olive oil. When the butter is lightly browned, add the shallot, reduce the heat to medium-low, and sauté just until soft and translucent, 2 to 3 minutes.

3. Add the peas and ½ cup water. Simmer, uncovered, until the peas are tender and the water has evaporated. Using a fork, roughly crush the peas in the sauté pan. Add the mint and season to taste with salt, pepper, and lemon juice.

4. Lightly brush both sides of the bread slices with olive oil and bake until golden brown. Spread the ricotta generously across each slice of bread and top with the pea mixture. Garnish with the grated pecorino and serve.

Roasted Pepper Tacos with Cream

Adapted from David Schuttenberg

TIME: *35 minutes*
YIELD: *4 to 6 tacos*

3 whole poblano peppers

1 tablespoon canola oil or other vegetable oil

2 tablespoons chopped cilantro leaves

1½ teaspoons fresh lime juice

¾ cup Mexican crema (crème fraîche may be substituted)

Four 8-inch or six 6-inch flour tortillas

In 1996, David Schuttenberg, a computer technician, met Christina Heath. She became his wife, but the person who sparked his passion for Mexican food—and the desire to cook it—was her mother, Cecilia Heath, who is Mexican.

"I learned Mexican cooking through my mother-in-law," said Mr. Schuttenberg, who was the chef and a partner at Cabrito, a Mexican restaurant in Greenwich Village, which has since closed. From her, he learned how to distinguish between one chile and another and how to make traditional sauces.

What she did not teach him was how to fill soft flour tortillas with strips of roasted poblanos and then swath them in crema—Mexican sour cream, or crème fraîche. He first ate the dish, *tacos con rajas y crema*, in 2004 at Mercadito, a Mexican restaurant in the East Village, whose chef and owner is Patricio Sandoval. At first bite, "I fell in love with it," Mr. Schuttenberg said. "I can't even remember the presentation. It was about the rich flavor, the rich crema and the bitter chiles." When he met the chef, he did not ask him how the tacos were prepared but went home and taught himself how to make it. The traditional dish was on the Cabrito menu.

"It's one of those dishes that is so comforting and kind of defines everything we were trying to do: soulful, easy, and deeply flavorful," Mr. Schuttenberg said. "I ashamedly admit to eating it several times a week."

{continued}

1. Using a gas stove or grill, place the peppers over an open flame, turning regularly, until roasted and charred all over. (Alternatively, the peppers may be roasted on a baking sheet under a broiler.) Immediately transfer to a bowl, cover with plastic wrap, and allow to steam for 15 minutes. Peel off the charred skin, remove the stems and seeds, and cut into long strips ½ inch wide.

2. Heat a medium skillet over medium-high heat. Add the oil and peppers. Sauté for 1 minute, then stir in the cilantro and lime juice. Add the crema and stir until heated. If the crema is thin, reduce until slightly thickened but still creamy, 1 to 2 minutes. If using crème fraîche, stir in and immediately remove the pan from the heat.

3. Heat a griddle or large skillet over medium-high heat. Heat the tortillas on the griddle until piping hot, turning once, 15 to 20 seconds on each side. To serve, place a tortilla on a warmed plate and add a serving of the pepper mixture. Fold the tortilla in half, gently flattening it, and serve immediately.

Hungarian Potato and Egg Casserole

Adapted from Sarabeth Levine

TIME: 1¹/₂ hours
YIELD: 4 servings

1¹/₂ pounds russet, Idaho, or
   other baking potatoes,
   unpeeled and scrubbed
   (about 5 medium)
Salt
2 tablespoons vegetable oil
1 pound onions, thinly sliced
   (about 2 large)
6 large eggs
1 tablespoon unsalted butter,
   at room temperature
Freshly ground black pepper
Sweet Hungarian paprika
2 cups sour cream
Green salad, for serving
   (optional)

Sarabeth Levine, the baker, restaurateur, and cookbook author, gave me the recipe for *rakott krumpli*, a Hungarian layered casserole of potatoes and eggs with sour cream and paprika, at a party. I was so excited by the simple and tasty sound of it that the moment I got home, I made it with one potato, one egg—and a tweak. I added a layer of sautéed onions to moisten and sweeten the dish.

It is delicious.

Ms. Levine learned it from her mother-in-law, Margaret Firestone, who was very religious and did not cook on the Jewish Sabbath until after sundown. Then she sometimes prepared the casserole as a dairy dinner. Ms. Levine said, "Margaret did not put onions in it."

Rakott krumpli is also a very popular dish in Hungary, where it is eaten as a main course, usually for supper, and sometimes with sausage, Ms. Levine said. "It also makes a fine brunch or breakfast dish, accompanied by a green salad."

1. Place the potatoes in a large pot and add enough cold, lightly salted water to cover by 2 inches. Bring to a boil over high heat. Cook until the potatoes are just tender, about 20 minutes. Drain and rinse under cold water until cool enough to handle. Peel the potatoes and cut into ¹/₂-inch rounds.

{continued}

2. Place a medium sauté pan over medium heat. Add the vegetable oil and heat until shimmering. Add the onions, and sauté until soft and almost caramelized, about 25 minutes; lower the heat if they begin to brown too quickly.

3. Place the eggs in a large pot and add enough cold water to cover by 2 inches. Bring to a boil over high heat, then reduce the heat to medium-low and simmer for 10 minutes. Drain and rinse under cold water until cool enough to handle. Peel the eggs and cut into 1/3-inch rounds.

4. Preheat the oven to 350°F. Generously coat the inside of a 1- to 1 1/2-quart baking dish with the butter. Arrange a layer of half the potatoes in the dish, then a layer of half the onions, and then a layer of half the eggs. Season with salt and pepper and a light sprinkling of paprika. Spread with half the sour cream. Repeat with the remaining potatoes, onions, and eggs, and season to taste with salt and pepper. Spread with the remaining sour cream and sprinkle with paprika.

5. Cover the baking dish and place in the center rack of the oven. Bake for 45 minutes. If desired, serve with a green salad.

Leek, Potato, and Zucchini Hotcakes
with Baby Lettuces and Lemon Vinaigrette

Adapted from James Laird,
Executive Chef-Owner, Restaurant Serenade

TIME: 1 1/2 hours
YIELD: 2 servings

FOR THE HOTCAKES:

8 ounces russet potato

Salt

3 whole leeks, white and light
　　green parts, sliced crosswise
　　into 1/8-inch-wide pieces
　　(to make about 4 cups)
　　and thoroughly rinsed

1 cup shredded zucchini

1 large egg, beaten

1/4 cup all-purpose flour

1/3 cup grated Parmesan
　　cheese

2 tablespoons chopped fresh
　　parsley leaves

Freshly ground black pepper

2 tablespoons canola or
　　olive oil

In the summer of 2010, James Laird, the executive chef and owner of Restaurant Serenade in Chatham, New Jersey, created savory potato pancakes mixed with blanched leeks and shredded zucchini, served with a salad of baby lettuces.

Leeks frustrate some cooks because they often contain a lot of sand. He has a solution to that: When they are cooked, he lifts them out of the water, rather than pouring them into a colander. That way, he said, the dirt goes to the bottom of the pot.

He also cooks them thoroughly. "Most people undercook leeks," he said. "Cook them all the way to bring out the natural sugar."

His salad dressing is as delightful as the pancakes. He mixes olive oil with lemon juice, salt, pepper, garlic, shallots, honey, and lemon zest. It has a bright, clean, light taste, and, since the summer, it has become my favorite salad dressing.

1. Preheat the oven to 400°F. Place the potato on a small baking pan and bake until tender in the center when pierced with a fork, about 1 hour. Allow to cool. Peel, discard the skin, and shred the potato on the large holes of a box grater. Set aside.

2. Bring a large pot of salted water to a boil. Add the leeks and blanch until tender, 4 to 5 minutes. Strain. Place the leeks in a dish

{continued}

Juice and finely grated zest
of 1 lemon

1 teaspoon honey

½ cup extra-virgin olive oil

1 garlic clove, peeled and
crushed

Salt and freshly ground
black pepper

3 cups fresh baby lettuces

1 small shallot, minced

towel, and twist firmly and repeatedly to remove the excess moisture; the leeks will shrink greatly. Set aside.

3. Place the zucchini in a bowl and sprinkle lightly with salt. Allow to sit for 10 minutes. Place the zucchini in a dish towel, and twist firmly and repeatedly to remove the excess moisture. The zucchini will shrink greatly. Set aside.

4. In a medium bowl, combine the potato, leeks, zucchini, egg, flour, cheese, and parsley. Season to taste with salt and pepper. Mix well. In a large skillet over medium heat, add the oil and heat until shimmering. Measure ¼ cup of the leek and potato mixture and form into a patty shape about ⅔ inch thick. Repeat with the remainder of the mixture.

5. Working in batches, if necessary, fry the cakes, flattening them with a spatula to ⅔ inch, until they are golden brown on each side, 4 to 5 minutes a side. Set aside and keep warm.

6. For the salad: In a medium jar, combine the lemon juice and zest, honey, and olive oil. Shake well to combine. Add the garlic and season to taste with salt and pepper. Shake again. In a salad bowl, combine the lettuces and shallot, and drizzle with the dressing to taste.

7. To serve, divide the hotcakes between two plates. Add equal portions of salad and serve.

Potato and Swiss Chard Gratin

Adapted from Jim Leiken, Executive Chef, DBGB Kitchen & Bar

TIME: 1 hour and 45 minutes
YIELD: 6 to 8 servings

Salt

1 pound Swiss chard leaves
and slender stems, stems
cut into 1/4-inch cubes

2 1/2 cups heavy cream

1 garlic clove, smashed

1 small shallot, sliced

2 sprigs thyme

1 bay leaf

1/4 teaspoon freshly grated
nutmeg

3 pounds (6 to 8 medium)
Yukon Gold potatoes, peeled

1 tablespoon butter, at room
temperature

Freshly ground black pepper

6 ounces grated Gruyère
cheese

Jim Leiken, the executive chef at DBGB Kitchen & Bar on the Bowery, which is part of the Daniel Boulud group of restaurants, was creating the fall menu, looking for a hearty, rustic garnish to go with the whole roast suckling pig. "I wanted an impressive presentation, but something that was fun to share for a big table of people. It's basically a potato gratin with some Swiss chard."

It is a celebratory, filling dish that can serve as the centerpiece of a meal.

Mr. Leiken said that some people are intimidated by the idea of making a gratin. If you are afraid of a mandoline, just use a sharp knife and slice the potatoes as thinly as you can. Few will notice if each slice is not a uniform 1/8 inch thick.

1. Preheat the oven to 350°F and place a rack in the center. Bring a large pot of lightly salted water to a boil; set a bowl of ice water on the side. Boil the Swiss chard leaves until tender, 3 to 5 minutes, then, using a slotted spoon, transfer to ice water to chill. Squeeze dry, chop roughly, and set aside. In the same pot of boiling water, boil the diced chard stems until tender, 3 to 5 minutes. Drain well and add to the chopped chard leaves.

2. In a small saucepan, combine the heavy cream, garlic, shallot, thyme, and bay leaf. Bring to a simmer and cook until reduced

{continued}

by half, about 25 minutes; strain and discard the solids. Stir in the nutmeg.

3. While the cream is reducing, using a mandoline or sharp knife, slice the potatoes into ⅛-inch-thick rounds. Grease a 12- to 14-inch gratin dish with butter. Assemble the gratin by layering the ingredients in this order: a single, slightly overlapping layer of one-third of the potato slices, a sprinkling of salt and pepper, one-third of the Gruyère, half of the Swiss chard, and one-third of the cream. Repeat once, and then top with one more layer of potato, salt and pepper, remaining Gruyère, and any remaining cream.

4. Bake until browned and the potatoes are tender when pierced with a fork, about 45 minutes or longer. Serve hot.

Spicy Potatoes (*Batata Harra*) (Vegan)

Adapted from Philippe G. Massoud,
Executive Chef and Co-Owner, Ilili

TIME: *1 hour, plus 2 hours'*
refrigeration
YIELD: *4 servings*

FOR THE POTATOES:

4 russet or Idaho potatoes,
   peeled

4 cups vegetable
   oil for deep-frying

FOR THE SAUCE:

1/4 cup extra-virgin olive oil

3 tablespoons minced garlic

1/2 cup plus 1 tablespoon
   minced cilantro

2 tablespoons Aleppo pepper
   (or substitute 1 3/4
   tablespoons paprika plus
   1 teaspoon cayenne)

Salt

2 tablespoons minced flat-leaf
   parsley

Batata Harra is a Lebanese dish of twice-fried potatoes. The crisp, golden cubes are served with a sauce of cilantro, garlic, and olive oil. "It's a poor man's dinner, eaten with eggs or with tomatoes and scallions," said Philippe G. Massoud, the executive chef and co-owner of Ilili, a Lebanese restaurant near Madison Square Park, in New York.

Mr. Massoud started cooking at the age of eight at his family's hotel, Coral Beach, in Beirut, and worked there until he was fourteen. That year, he came to the United States to visit an aunt in Scarsdale, New York, and stayed on. "That was 1985, ten years after the civil war started, and my parents told me not to go back." His aunt became his legal guardian.

Over the course of his cooking career, he worked at restaurants in Manhattan, at places like Carmine's and The Saloon near Lincoln Center, and in Washington, D.C., where he helped develop Neyla, a Mediterranean restaurant named after his sister and one of the investor's daughters, who shared the name.

Six years ago, he returned to Manhattan, and in 2007, he finally opened his own place, Ilili, which translates to "tell me" in the colloquial Arabic spoken in Lebanon.

1. Cut the potatoes into 1/2-inch cubes. Rinse under cold water until the water runs clear. Drain and dry thoroughly on paper towels.

{continued}

2 tablespoons fresh lemon
     juice
Sliced tomatoes and scallions
     or fried, scrambled, or
     poached eggs, for serving

2. Pour the oil into a deep fryer or a large, deep, frying pan to a 2-inch depth. Heat the oil to 300°F. Set aside a baking sheet lined with paper towels. Working in batches, if necessary, fry the potatoes until tender inside, about 5 minutes. Transfer the potatoes from the oil to the baking sheet. Turn off the fryer, or if using a pan, remove from the stove but do not discard the oil.

3. Allow the potatoes to cool to room temperature, then refrigerate uncovered for 2 hours. Meanwhile, prepare the sauce.

4. Heat the ¼ cup olive oil in a wide saucepan over medium-low heat. Stir in the garlic, cover, and reduce the heat to low. Cook, stirring occasionally, until soft and pale gold, about 3 minutes; do not allow to brown. Add the cilantro and stir until wilted, 1 to 2 minutes. Remove from the heat, transfer to a large mixing bowl, and set aside.

5. Remove the potatoes from the refrigerator and allow to come to room temperature. Meanwhile, heat the deep fryer or frying pan to 350 to 375°F. Set aside a baking sheet lined with paper towels. Pat the potatoes with paper towels to be sure they are completely dry. Working in batches, if necessary, fry the potatoes again, this time until crisp and golden, 3 minutes or as needed. Transfer the potatoes from the oil to the baking sheet.

6. When all the potatoes are cooked, add to the bowl of sauce, sprinkle with Aleppo pepper and salt to taste, and toss gently. Transfer the mixture to a serving bowl and garnish with minced parsley. Drizzle with lemon juice. If desired, serve with sliced tomatoes and scallions or with fried, scrambled, or poached eggs.

Potato Tortilla

Adapted from Eder Montero, Co-Chef and Co-Owner, Txikito

TIME: 25 minutes
YIELD: 4 servings

3 large Idaho or other baking
   potatoes, peeled and
   quartered lengthwise,
   then thinly sliced crosswise
3 cups delicate-flavored
   Spanish olive oil
1 tablespoon plus 1 teaspoon
   salt, or to taste
½ medium white onion,
   thinly sliced
4 large eggs
Mayonnaise, for serving
   (optional)

Eder Montero would like to set one thing straight regarding potato tortillas: They should not be as brown as, well, a plate of hash browns.

"Tortillas classically should have very little color," said Mr. Montero, who is a chef and an owner of Txikito, a Basque restaurant in Chelsea. A pale golden yellow is more like it.

What gives the tortilla its elusive flavor is that the potatoes and onions are submerged in gently bubbling olive oil—three cups of it in this recipe. "The only expensive ingredient is the olive oil," the chef said.

But he points out that you can refrigerate the used olive oil for your next tortilla or to sauté vegetables another day.

The tortilla is "an old dish, and found all over Spain, in every district, and is offered as a tapa, or served at home for lunch or dinner as a main course with a salad or roasted peppers," Mr. Montero said.

It can be eaten hot or cold, and is good the next day. When it's cold, the chef eats it by itself, with mayonnaise on the side, or as the filling of a carbohydrate-on-carbohydrate sandwich.

"If you have to reheat it, do it at 350°F for five minutes, just to take the chill away," he said. "If you heat it too much, it will get dry."

At Txikito, potato tortillas are often on the menu as specials. Lucky employees sometimes get to eat them at the staff dinner.

{continued}

1. Spread the potatoes in a heavy flameproof casserole, cover with olive oil, and sprinkle with salt. Spread the onion on top. Place over medium-high heat until the oil bubbles. Reduce the heat and simmer, stirring gently once or twice, until the potatoes are tender but not broken, 7 to 10 minutes.

2. Place a mesh colander over a heatproof bowl, and drain the potatoes and onion, reserving the oil. In a large bowl, whisk the eggs until frothy. Add the potato mixture to the eggs and stir gently to combine.

3. Place an 8-inch nonstick pan or well-seasoned skillet over medium-high heat. Add 3 tablespoons reserved olive oil. Add one-third of the potato mixture and stir with a wooden spoon or spatula. Cook until the egg is barely set, about 30 seconds. Reduce the heat to medium-low. Add another third of the mixture and stir for 15 seconds. Add the remaining third and stir two or three times. Gently pat the mixture to flatten it, and allow it to sit until the top is loose, the center is somewhat firm, and the bottom is firm (pale golden, not golden brown), about 30 seconds.

4. Run a spatula around the perimeter of the tortilla, shaking the pan to be sure the edges and bottom are free. Place a small flat plate that fits securely inside the pan directly on top of the tortilla. Wearing a kitchen mitt, grasp the handle close to the pan. In one quick movement, flip the tortilla onto the plate.

5. Quickly wipe out the pan, add 2 tablespoons reserved olive oil, and return the pan to medium-low heat until reheated. Slide the tortilla back into the reheated pan so the bottom is now the top. Pat down to compact the layers of potatoes and eliminate air bubbles. When the tortilla is set and the bottom and edges are free of the pan, use the spatula or a spoon to turn in the edges to give the tortilla a more compact, attractive shape. If desired, the tortilla can be allowed to rest for 5 minutes on the lowest possible heat before it is turned onto a serving plate.

6. To serve, slice the hot tortilla into large wedges. It may also be covered and refrigerated for up to 24 hours, then served cold with mayonnaise.

Sweet Potato and Goat Cheese Gratin with Black Olives

*Adapted from Sisha Ortuzar,
Chef, Riverpark, and Partner, 'wichcraft*

TIME: 1 hour and 45 minutes
YIELD: 4 side-dish servings

2 pounds sweet potatoes
  or yams
¼ cup niçoise olives, pitted
3 ounces unsalted butter
1 large shallot, finely chopped
Kosher salt and freshly ground
  black pepper to taste
3 to 4 ounces creamy fresh
  goat cheese
2 tablespoons olive oil
4 to 5 basil leaves,
  finely chopped

This sweet potato and goat cheese gratin, sprinkled with crispy black olives, started life in a slightly different variation, as a sandwich, said Sisha Ortuzar, chef at Riverpark and a partner with Tom Colicchio at 'wichcraft. "I introduced it in 2008 as a sandwich with pumpkin, mozzarella, hazelnuts, and brown butter."

It is a very rich and nicely textured version of that holiday basic: mashed sweet potatoes.

The small culinary revelation is that if you bake the niçoise olives in a little bit of olive oil they will become brittle. "You've taken the water out," Mr. Ortuzar said.

1. Preheat the oven to 350°F. If you are using an aluminum baking sheet, cover the bottom with parchment paper or Silpat so that the potatoes won't discolor and turn brown while baking. If you are using a ceramic or stainless-steel baking sheet, you don't need to cover the bottom. Slice each sweet potato in half lengthwise, and place cut-side-down on the tray. Bake until they are soft, about 35 to 45 minutes. Remove and allow to cool.

2. Increase the heat in the oven to 400°F. Place the pitted olives on a small baking sheet, and bake until they become hard and brittle, about 20 to 25 minutes.

3. While the olives are baking, place a medium-sized sauté pan with a heavy bottom over medium heat. Add the butter, and brown it until it turns a hazelnut color and has a nutty fragrance, about 5 to 6 minutes. Add the chopped shallot and allow to cook for about 3 minutes, until translucent. Be careful not to burn the butter.

4. When the sweet potatoes are cool, scoop out the insides and place in a bowl. Pour the butter and shallot mixture over the sweet potatoes, and mix. Season with salt and pepper to taste, going lightly on the salt since the olives, which are added at the end, are salty. Place the sweet potato mixture in a baking dish so that the sweet potatoes are 1 inch thick. Spread the creamy goat cheese in shallow dollops over the sweet potatoes, so that the sweet potatoes are clearly visible at the edges, and elsewhere. Bake at 400°F, or until the cheese and potatoes start to brown in some spots, about 15 minutes. The gratin won't brown like a traditional potato gratin; the colors of the sweet potatoes and the goat cheese will still be very present, but the goat cheese will turn beige and the potatoes will begin to brown a bit.

5. Once the olives are cool, chop them finely, and mix with the olive oil and the chopped basil. Spoon the olive mixture over the hot goat cheese and serve.

Roast Pumpkin and Watercress Salad

Adapted from Natalia Machado,
Executive Chef, Industria Argentina

TIME: 1 hour
YIELD: 2 large or 4 small servings

FOR THE PUMPKIN:

12 ounces pumpkin or
   butternut or other winter
   squash, peeled, seeded,
   and cut into ½-inch cubes

1 teaspoon salt

1 teaspoon sugar

½ teaspoon chopped fresh
   thyme

1 garlic clove, finely minced

2 tablespoons extra-virgin
   olive oil

FOR THE CHEESE CRACKERS:

Vegetable oil or nonstick spray

8 tablespoons grated
   Parmesan cheese or
   Argentine Reggianito

This brilliantly colored salad—orange roasted pumpkin atop emerald green watercress with a pesto dressing—is Natalia Machado's homage to her mother (who loved watercress), the American seasons (the pumpkin), and the Italians (the pesto). The executive chef of Industria Argentina in TriBeCa tops off the salad with a cheese cracker, which is nothing more than a grated mound of Argentine Reggianito or Parmesan melted in the oven until almost crisp, then scooped off and cooled. Making the crispy, lacy cheese cracker requires vigilance.

1. For the pumpkin: Preheat the oven to 375°F. On a baking sheet, toss the pumpkin with the salt, sugar, thyme, garlic, and 2 tablespoons olive oil. Roast until tender and lightly browned, 15 to 25 minutes. Remove from the heat and set aside; do not turn off the oven.

2. While the pumpkin is roasting, prepare the cheese crackers: On a nonstick or lightly oiled cookie sheet, divide the grated Parmesan or Argentine Reggianito cheese into four equal mounds placed about 3 inches apart. Bake until the cheese has melted, turned lightly golden, and set into a cracker; watch carefully to prevent burning. Remove from the oven, and using a spatula, gently loosen the crackers from the cookie sheet and set aside on a plate. Let the crackers cool and become crisp.

FOR THE DRESSING:

1 cup (lightly packed) roughly
    chopped fresh basil leaves

1 garlic clove, peeled

¼ cup grated Parmesan
    cheese or Argentine
    Reggianito

¼ cup extra-virgin olive oil

2 tablespoons white balsamic
    or apple cider vinegar

FOR ASSEMBLY:

3 cups watercress, large stems
    removed

3. For the dressing: In a blender, combine the basil, garlic, Parmesan or Argentine Reggianito, and ¼ cup olive oil. Process until smooth. Transfer to a small bowl and add the vinegar, mixing well. Set aside.

4. For assembly: In a large bowl, combine the watercress and dressing, and toss until all the leaves are coated. Place equal portions on two or four plates. Top with the roasted pumpkin and garnish with the cheese crackers.

R

Raclette

*Adapted from Terrance Brennan,
Chef-Owner, Artisanal and Picholine*

TIME: *40 minutes*
YIELD: *4 servings*

1 pound fingerling potatoes
  (about 12)
1 tablespoon kosher salt,
  or as needed
10 ounces raclette or hard
  mountain cheeses like
  Emmentaler or Gruyère,
  thinly sliced
Freshly ground black pepper
2 scallions, trimmed and sliced
  diagonally in ⅛-inch strips
Cornichons, pickled onions, or
  pickled cauliflower (optional)
Green salad, for serving
  (optional)

Years ago, Terrance Brennan, the chef-owner of both Artisanal and Picholine in Manhattan, was in Gruyères, Switzerland, and ate his first raclette. The dish is named after a firm cow cheese used in this almost too-simple but nevertheless hearty, tasty dish of melted cheese on cooked potato slices.

"The cheese is held in a vise of curved metal," he said, "and you put the vise 12 inches from the fire, and push it back and forth, so the cheese melts." The server scrapes the melted cheese onto a plate that holds cooked potatoes and cornichons.

For the home cook, Mr. Brennan created a version that can be finished off in the oven in minutes. You slice cooked potatoes, drape the warm potatoes with thin slices of raclette (or Gruyère or Comté or Emmentaler) and put them in the oven until the cheese melts. He suggests serving a raclette with cornichons, other kinds of pickled vegetables, or a salad.

The home version differs from what he ate in Switzerland only in ambiance. "It's not as romantic as a fire," he said.

At Artisanal, if raclette is not on the menu, a customer may request it. "We have potatoes, and we have cheese," he said.

1. In a large pot, combine 8 cups water, the potatoes, and 1 tablespoon salt. Place over high heat to bring to a boil, then reduce the heat to low and simmer until the potatoes are tender when pierced with a fork, 15 to 25 minutes. Drain and set aside.

{*continued*}

2. If you have ovenproof plates, preheat a broiler. If you do not have ovenproof plates, preheat the oven to 250°F. When cool enough to handle, cut the potatoes in half lengthwise. Divide the warm potatoes, cut-side up, evenly among four plates, arranging them in a pinwheel pattern.

3. Arrange one-quarter of the cheese slices in a single layer over each portion of potatoes, taking care to completely cover all the potatoes. Broil or bake until the cheese melts, about 3 minutes in a broiler or 10 minutes in an oven.

4. Season with salt and pepper to taste. Serve hot, garnished with scallions sprinkled on top. Cornichons, pickled onions, and pickled cauliflower are optional accompaniments. If desired, the dish may be served with a green salad.

Ratatouille with Tom Yum Sauce (Vegan)

Adapted from Irene Khin Wong,
Director, Saffron 59 Catering and Consultancy

TIME: 1 hour and 15 minutes
YIELD: 4 servings

FOR THE ROASTED VEGETABLES:

1 small cauliflower (about 1½ pounds), cut into 1½-inch florets

2 medium carrots, peeled and sliced diagonally into 1-inch chunks

1 medium Asian eggplant (about ¾ pound), trimmed and cut diagonally into 1-inch-thick slices

1 large red bell pepper, cored, seeded, and cut into 1½-inch squares

1 small yellow summer squash, cut diagonally into 1-inch-thick slices

2 tablespoons olive oil

Salt and freshly ground black pepper

This dish—ratatouille with tom yum broth—may sound like a French fusion dish, but it is not. It consists of roasted vegetables—cauliflower, carrots, eggplant, squash, and sweet pepper—in a sauce that combines both Thai and Indian flavors. "The ground coriander, cumin, and turmeric are Indian, and the broth, with the tom yum paste, is very Thai," said Irene Khin Wong, the director of Saffron 59 Catering and Consultancy in Manhattan, who is herself Burmese. "Neither the Indians nor the Thais roast the vegetables, but the roasting gives the vegetables a nice firm bite."

It is a dish for all seasons. "It's easygoing and inexpensive," Ms. Wong said. "You can make the broth and roast the vegetables a day before, and put it together when the guests arrive." She said that if you keep the dish refrigerated but keep the broth and vegetables separate, it can be stored for up to three days.

1. For the roasted vegetables: Preheat the oven to 350°F. Sprinkle the cauliflower, carrots, eggplant, pepper, and squash with the olive oil, salt, and pepper. Mix well. Place the vegetables, organizing them by kind, in a roasting pan, so if some vegetables cook more quickly than others they can be removed easily. Roast until crisp-tender, 20 to 30 minutes, removing them as they are ready. Set aside, or cool, cover, and refrigerate up to 24 hours.

{continued}

FOR THE SAUCE:

2 tablespoons vegetable oil

1 medium onion, diced

1 tablespoon minced garlic

1 tablespoon minced ginger

1½ teaspoons curry powder

1½ teaspoons ground cumin

1½ teaspoons paprika

1½ teaspoons turmeric

Pinch of cayenne

³/₄ pound tomatoes,
   cut into ¼-inch dice

2 cups vegetable broth

1 teaspoon chile paste in
   soybean oil

2 teaspoons tom yum paste

Salt and freshly ground
   black pepper

Juice from half a lime

10 cilantro leaves, for garnish

Mango chutney (optional)

Cooked rice, for serving
   (optional)

2. For the sauce: Place a large skillet over medium heat and heat the oil until shimmering. Add the onion, garlic, and ginger, and sauté until the onion is translucent and turning golden, about 10 minutes. Add the curry, cumin, paprika, turmeric, and cayenne, and stir for 1 minute. Add the diced tomatoes and vegetable broth. Simmer, uncovered, stirring often and scraping the bottom of the pan, for 10 minutes.

3. In a small bowl, mix the chile paste and tom yum paste. Add the mixed pastes and roasted vegetables to the sauce. Reduce the heat to low, and simmer until the vegetables are tender and have absorbed the flavor of the sauce, about 10 minutes. Season with salt and pepper to taste. Serve hot, topped with a sprinkle of lime juice and cilantro. If desired, accompany with mango chutney as a condiment and serve with rice.

99 LBS. NET WEIGHT

TABLE RICE

R

for rice

Creamy Rice Casserole

Adapted from Zarela Martinez, Cookbook Author

TIME: 1¹/₂ hours
YIELD: 4 servings

2 teaspoons butter

1 teaspoon salt

1 cup Uncle Ben's
   or other converted rice

1 poblano chile

¹/₂ cup sour cream

¹/₈ cup plus ¹/₄ cup
   chopped onion

2 tablespoons
   chopped cilantro

Salt

1 tablespoon vegetable oil

1 garlic clove, minced

1 cup fresh or frozen
   corn kernels

¹/₈ cup fresh or frozen peas

4 ounces grated Cheddar
   cheese

Green salad, for serving
   (optional)

This rice casserole, studded with fresh corn kernels, peas, and a poblano chile and made creamy with sour cream and Cheddar cheese, is Mexican comfort food. "People love it because it's creamy, crunchy, and cheesy," said Zarela Martinez, the owner and founding chef of Zarela's restaurant in Manhattan, which is now closed. and a cookbook author. "It's Mexican baby food. Like rice and beans." In 2010 she said that her preschool-age granddaughter, Violeta, eats it.

But it is also a party dish.

"It was the first catered dish I ever had, in Juarez, Chihuahua," Ms. Martinez said. "I went to boarding school across the border in El Paso, Texas. The chef's name was Chonito, and he served this dish at every party he catered.

"This is definitely a Chihuahua dish," she said. "There are versions of it in other places. The variations might just have corn or not have cream. What they always have is cheese and poblano."

Before roasting the poblano, Ms. Martinez suggests making a 1-inch-long vertical cut in the chile. "Or it may explode," she said.

1. Preheat the oven broiler. In a small saucepan, bring 2 cups water to a boil and add the butter and salt. When the butter is melted, add the rice and return to a boil. Reduce the heat to very low, cover the rice with a tight-fitting lid, and cook 25 to 30 minutes. Spread the rice on a baking sheet to cool. (To cool quickly, put the rice on

{continued}

the baking sheet in the freezer for 10 to 15 minutes, stirring every 5 minutes.)

2. Place the poblano on a broiling pan about 2 inches from the broiler. Using a pair of tongs, turn the poblano every 3 to 5 minutes, until blistered all over, about 15 minutes. (Alternatively, the poblano may be roasted directly over a gas flame, turning every minute until blistered all over, 3 to 5 minutes.) Transfer to a paper bag and allow to cool. Reduce the oven temperature to 350°F.

3. When the poblano is cool enough to handle, gently scrape away the blistered outer skin and discard the top. Slice open lengthwise and gently scrape away and discard the seeds. Slice lengthwise in 1/4-inch strips and cut crosswise into 1/4-inch dice. In a small bowl, combine the sour cream, 1/8 cup chopped onion, and the chopped cilantro. Season with salt to taste.

4. In a skillet over medium heat, heat the vegetable oil until shimmering. Add 1/4 cup chopped onion and the garlic. Sauté until translucent, 1 to 2 minutes. Add the diced poblano and sauté 1 minute, then remove from the heat and transfer to a casserole or clay pot. Add the rice, corn, and peas. Toss lightly. Add the sour cream mixture and grated cheese. Mix lightly but thoroughly. Cover the casserole or clay pot with a lid or foil; if using a Pyrex casserole, reduce the oven temperature to 325°F. Bake until thoroughly heated, about 30 minutes. Serve with a green salad, if desired.

Five Vegetables and Fifteen-Grain Rice Pot (Vegan)

Adapted from Abe Hiroki, Executive Chef, EN Japanese Brasserie

TIME: 1 hour, plus 1 to 3 hours' soaking time for mushrooms
YIELD: 4 servings

4 large dried shiitake
   mushrooms
1 tablespoon sake
1 tablespoon mirin
2 teaspoons soy sauce
1¼ cups 15-grain rice,
   rinsed until water
   runs clear
2 tablespoons burdock
   root, peeled, soaked in
   cold water for 15 minutes,
   drained, and julienned
1 tablespoon dry hijiki
   seaweed, soaked in warm
   water for 10 minutes,
   drained, and julienned
2 tablespoons julienned
   carrots

This Japanese rice pot made with mushrooms, carrots, edamame, burdock, and seaweed is an austere, quietly flavored dish, with equally subtle textures. It's the dish that Abe Hiroki, the executive chef at EN Japanese Brasserie, ate as a child growing up in Fukuoka City, on the island of Kyushu.

Mr. Hiroki recommends asking for fifteen-grain rice, or jugokoku-mai, which comes in small packets at Japanese food stores. Online, you can purchase six-grain rice. If you have only white rice on hand, you can simply add the five vegetables.

Regardless of what rice you use, the dish is a brilliant foil to a salad with a sprightly dressing and topped with crunchy nuts. EN Brasserie suggests accompanying it with an asparagus salad and pickled vegetables, such as carrots, cucumbers, and radish. For those who like their grains packed with walloping flavor, this is not for you. For those who equate food, now and then, with meditation, this is for you.

1. Place the shiitake mushrooms in a medium bowl and cover with 2¼ cups water. Allow to soak 1 to 3 hours. Remove the mushrooms, reserving the liquid, and squeeze the mushrooms over the bowl. Remove and discard the mushroom stems, and slice the mushrooms into ¼-inch strips.

{continued}

2 tablespoons frozen shelled
  edamame
Toasted sesame seeds,
  for garnish
Japanese pickled sliced
  daikon, hijiki, cucumbers,
  or green salad, for serving
  (optional)

2. In a medium-sized (about 4 quarts) clay pot (or other kind of pot) over medium heat, combine 1¼ cups reserved mushroom liquid, the sake, mirin, and soy sauce. Add the rice and stir gently. Top the rice with the mushrooms, burdock, hijiki, carrots, and edamame; do not stir.

3. Cover and raise the heat to bring to a boil. Reduce the heat to low and simmer for 16 minutes. Turn off the heat and leave covered for 8 minutes. Using a spatula, fluff up the rice and garnish with a sprinkling of sesame seeds. If desired, serve accompanied by Japanese pickled sliced daikon, hijiki, cucumbers, or a green salad.

Korean Rice Pot (*Bibimbap*) (Vegan)

Adapted from Eleazar Martinez,
Executive Chef, Bann and Woo Lae Oak Soho

TIME: *About 1 hour*
YIELD: *4 servings*

1 cup short-grain rice,
   rinsed well and drained

1 medium zucchini, julienned,
   in 2-inch lengths

Salt

3 1/2 teaspoons dark
   sesame oil

1/2 teaspoon minced garlic

1/2 teaspoon sugar,
   plus a pinch

1 teaspoon toasted sesame
   seeds, plus a pinch

1 cup thinly sliced shiitake
   mushroom caps

1/2 teaspoon soy sauce

1 cup bean sprouts

1 cup packed spinach leaves

1 cup peeled and julienned
   daikon radish, in 2-inch
   lengths

At two Korean restaurants in Manhattan, Bann and Woo Lae Oak Soho, the *bibimbap* follows the recipe of Eleazar Martinez, a Honduran-born chef.

How did someone who grew up making soups out of oxtail, tripe, or conch end up a master of the traditional Korean casserole of vegetables (and often meat or egg) atop crisp, golden shards of fried rice?

Being flexible, curious, and hungry helped. In 1990, when he was twenty-four, Mr. Martinez moved to Los Angeles from his hometown of San Pedro Sula; he had cooked in his aunt's small hotel there, and had also become a certified public accountant, but couldn't find work as a C.P.A.

In Los Angeles, he found a job as a busboy at the Korean restaurant Woo Lae Oak, and after three months, he said, "My boss, Mrs. Young Sook Choi, asked me if I wanted to try to cook." In 1999, Mrs. Choi, the owner, sent him to New York to open Woo Lae Oak Soho, where he was the first sous-chef. Then she sent him to the New York Restaurant School from 2001 to 2002, while he also cooked part-time. In 2003, he spent a year in Seoul, learning the traditional dishes once made for the Korean court.

"*Bibimbap* was one of the first things I learned," said Mr. Martinez, who said that in Korea, it is often served with a fried egg on top, but not necessarily with beef or chicken, which are more expensive.

{continued}

1 teaspoon dried hot chile
flakes

1 teaspoon vegetable oil

¼ cup peeled and julienned
carrot, in 2-inch lengths

1 tablespoon Korean red chile
sauce (*gochujang*) or other
hot chile sauce, more to
taste

His vegetarian *bibimbap* respects tradition: It is lightly flavored with sesame oil, sesame seeds, minced garlic, sugar, and chile flakes. Home cooks can serve it, hot and sizzling, in the pan at the table.

Mr. Martinez now prefers Korean food to Latin food. "I like the freshness of the vegetables," he said, "and I identify with the sweet and spicy in Korean food—a little sugar, a little chile flakes, a little sesame seed, and sesame oil."

When he started at Woo Lae Oak nearly twenty years ago, he was the first Hispanic cook. Now, as executive chef of the two New York restaurants, he has assembled a staff of thirty cooks, all of whom come from Mexico, Ecuador, El Salvador, or Guatemala.

"I explain the recipes in Spanish," he said. "Then the cooks make the dish their own."

1. Place the rice in a medium saucepan and add 2 cups water. Place over high heat to bring to a boil, then reduce the heat to low. Cover and cook until the water is absorbed, about 25 minutes. Set aside.

2. While the rice cooks, place another medium pot of water over high heat to bring to a boil. Place the zucchini in a colander and sprinkle with 1 teaspoon salt; set aside to drain for 10 minutes. Rinse and pat dry with paper towels.

3. Place a medium skillet over medium heat, and add 1 teaspoon sesame oil and ¼ teaspoon garlic. Add the zucchini, a pinch of sugar, and ½ teaspoon sesame seeds. Sauté 2 minutes, then transfer to a plate; set aside. Wipe out the pan and return to medium heat. Add 1 teaspoon sesame oil and the remaining ¼ teaspoon garlic. Add the shiitakes, a pinch of salt, and the soy sauce. Sauté 2 minutes, then transfer to a plate; set aside.

4. Place the bean sprouts in the boiling water until wilted, about 20 seconds. Using a slotted spoon, transfer to the colander to drain. Place the sprouts in a bowl, and add $\frac{1}{2}$ teaspoon sesame oil, a pinch of salt, and a pinch of sesame seeds; set aside. Add the spinach to the pot of boiling water, and blanch until it wilts and turns bright green, about 30 seconds. Drain into the colander, rinse well with cold water until chilled, then drain, squeezing out the excess water. Transfer to a bowl and add $\frac{1}{4}$ teaspoon salt, $\frac{1}{2}$ teaspoon sesame oil, and $\frac{1}{2}$ teaspoon sesame seeds. Mix well and set aside. Place the daikon in a bowl, and add the hot chile flakes, $\frac{1}{2}$ teaspoon sugar, $\frac{1}{2}$ teaspoon sesame oil, and a pinch of salt. Mix well and set aside.

5. Place a 9-inch well-seasoned cast-iron or nonstick skillet over medium heat. Add 1 teaspoon vegetable oil and heat until shimmering. Add 1 cup cooked rice and flatten it to form a pancake covering the bottom of the pan, about $\frac{1}{3}$ inch thick. Cook until it is crisp and golden on the underside, about 5 minutes. Use a large spatula to flip it over, and cook again until crisp, another 5 minutes. Break the crusty rice into several pieces. Add the remaining rice. Arrange the vegetables on top in wedge-shaped piles (like pizza slices), topping with the julienned carrot. Cook, uncovered, until well heated through, 10 to 15 minutes. Bring the skillet to the table, add the chile sauce, and toss the mixture gently to combine the ingredients. Serve hot.

NOTE: The vegetables may be prepared and stored, covered and refrigerated, for up to 2 days before serving.

Lemon Rice (Vegan)

Adapted from Suvir Saran, Executive Chef and an Owner, Devi

TIME: 1¹/₂ hours
YIELDS: 4 to 6 servings

1¹/₂ cups basmati rice,
 rinsed until water runs clear
2 tablespoons canola oil
1¹/₂ teaspoons black
 mustard seeds
1²/₃ cups roasted peanuts,
 preferably American
4 whole dried red Thai bird
 chiles, or half or omitted,
 if you want it medium
 or mild
¹/₂ teaspoon cumin seeds
¹/₂ teaspoon turmeric
8 fresh or 12 frozen
 curry leaves, torn into
 pieces
Pinch of asafetida (optional)
²/₃ cup golden raisins
²/₃ large red onion, halved
 through the root end,
 each half cut in half
 again crosswise and cut
 into ¹/₄-inch-thick slices

Lemon rice is an Indian fried rice, made crunchy with peanuts, spicy with mustard seeds and dried Thai bird chiles, and pale yellow with turmeric and lemon juice.

Suvir Saran, the executive chef and an owner of Devi in Manhattan, first ate it as a child in Nagpur, India, in the central part of the country. "The peanuts add a great amount of texture, flavor, and nutrition value to the rice," he said. "The raisins bring a sweetness to contrast with the nutty flavor of the peanuts and the heat of the spices.

"American peanuts are my favorite for several reasons," he said. "They are fresher, tastier, and more sustainable," in that they are relatively local. "I use Virginia peanuts—my favorite brand is Royal Oak—and when I want to add a little extra color to the rice, I use Valencia peanuts from New Mexico, with their skin on."

It is an easy dish to prepare, especially if you have leftover rice.

1. Place 3 cups water in a small saucepan, and bring to a boil. Add the rice and stir gently until it returns to a boil. Reduce the heat to low, cover, and simmer until the water is absorbed, 18 to 20 minutes. Uncover, spread on a baking sheet, and cool to room temperature.

2. Place a large frying pan or wok over medium-high heat. Add the oil and heat until shimmering. Add the mustard seeds and stir 1 to 2 minutes until the seeds begin to crackle and pop. Add the peanuts and stir 2 minutes. Add the chiles (if using), cumin seeds, turmeric, curry leaves, and asafetida (if using). Stir until the peanuts turn uniformly brown,

1/3 cup chopped scallion
   (use the white part and about
   2 inches of the green)
3/4 teaspoon salt, or to taste
Juice of 1 or 2 lemons,
   or as needed
Lemon or lime wedges,
   for serving (optional)

about 5 minutes. Add the raisins, onion, scallion, and salt. Sauté until the onion is translucent, about 5 minutes.

3. Add the cooled rice and stir gently, so as not to break the grains, until almost uniformly yellow. (Some white patches add to the dazzle of this dish.) Drizzle 2 tablespoons water all around the rim of the pan and stir again, gently scraping the bottom. Add the lemon juice and cook, uncovered, until the rice is warmed through, about 2 more minutes. Stir gently once or twice during cooking, scraping the bottom of the pan to keep the spices from sticking. Taste for lemon and salt. Garnish with lemon or lime wedges, if desired, and serve hot.

Vegetable Rice (*Arroz de Verduras*) (Vegan)

Adapted from George Mendes, Chef and Co-Owner, Aldea

TIME: 1 hour
YIELD: 6 to 8 servings

FOR THE SOFRITO :

2 large tomatoes

3 tablespoons olive oil

½ cup finely chopped onion

6 garlic cloves, finely
   chopped

Generous pinch of
   saffron threads

2 tablespoons sweet
   smoked paprika

FOR THE RICE:

⅓ cup olive oil

1 pound rice, preferably
   Bomba or Calasparra

4½ cups vegetable stock

2 cups carrots,
   cut into ⅓- to ½-inch dice

1 cup edamame

1 cup peas

2 cups corn kernels

¼ cup pitted kalamata olives,
   roughly chopped

Arroz de Verduras, or Vegetable Rice, is an intensely flavored dish of many colors. It is rice cooked in a sofrito, a base of garlic, onions, sweet paprika, fresh tomato, and saffron, and then studded with corn, edamame, peas, and olives and baked until the edges are crisp and golden. It is a dish with Portuguese roots that George Mendes, the chef and a co-owner of Aldea in Manhattan, introduced at his restaurant. As a first-generation American, he grew up in Danbury, Connecticut, surrounded by thirty relatives, all of whom had emigrated from Portugal. "My mom and my aunts all cooked," he said.

The base of the dish is a Spanish rice, either Calasparra or Bomba, the brands of rice used in a paella. "It absorbs so much flavor," Mr. Mendes said.

1. For the sofrito: Bring a pan of water to a boil, add the tomatoes, and blanch for 15 seconds. Drain, rinse under cold water, and peel. Core, seed, and cut into ½-inch dice. In a skillet over medium-low heat, add the oil and sauté the onion and garlic until golden. Add the saffron and sauté 2 minutes. Add the tomatoes and sauté until all the moisture is gone. Stir in the paprika and remove from the heat.

2. For the rice: In a large heavy-bottomed pot, combine the sofrito and olive oil. Place over medium-low heat. Add the rice and stir constantly with a wooden spoon or rubber spatula until the rice is toasted, about 1 minute. Add 3 cups stock and mix well. Simmer 10 minutes, stirring occasionally to prevent sticking. (At this point the

Salt and freshly ground
 black pepper
1/4 cup chopped flat-leaf
 parsley
1/4 cup chopped cilantro

rice is partially cooked and may be spread on a parchment-lined baking sheet, covered with more parchment, and allowed to sit at room temperature for up to 3 hours before finishing.)

3. To finish: Preheat the oven to 375°F. Bring a small pan of water to a boil, add the carrots, and blanch for 10 seconds. Drain and rinse with cold water. Spread the rice evenly across the bottom of a 16- to 18-inch paella or sauté pan, and scatter the edamame, peas, corn, carrots, and olives on top. Season to taste with salt and pepper. Drizzle with the remaining 1 1/2 cups stock.

4. Place the pan in the oven and bake until the rice is crisped around the edges and a *soccarat,* a crust, has formed on the bottom of the pan, about 20 minutes. Remove from the oven, cover with foil, and allow to rest for 5 minutes. Sprinkle with the chopped parsley and cilantro. Mix well, scraping the bottom and sides of the pan, and adjust the salt and pepper as desired. Serve hot.

Tomato, Oregano, and Feta Risotto

Adapted from Diane Kochilas, Consulting Chef, Pylos Restaurant

TIME: 1 hour and 15 minutes
YIELD: 4 servings

3 tablespoons extra-virgin
  olive oil
1 medium onion,
  finely chopped
Salt
2 garlic cloves, finely chopped
4 to 5 cups vegetable broth
1 cup carnaroli or arborio rice
1/3 cup ouzo
1 1/3 cups grated ripe tomato
  (see Note)
2/3 cup creamy feta, such as
  Dodoni or Cephalonia,
  or a French feta
2 tablespoons finely chopped
  fresh oregano leaves
Finely grated zest of 1 lemon
Freshly ground black pepper

This glorious pale red creamy risotto is Greek by way of Italy.

"It's a contemporary Greek dish inspired by something I tasted in a restaurant along the Attica coast, long gone now," said Diane Kochilas, the consulting chef at Pylos restaurant in Manhattan and a cookbook author who divides her time between New York and Greece. "Risotto is a new phenomenon here, definitely inspired by Italian cooking. It's a sort of hybrid dish. Rice is, of course, ancient, but not so much so in Greece. It was, until fairly recently, a luxury food."

1. In a large, deep skillet over medium-low heat, heat the olive oil until shimmering. Add the onion and a little salt and stir until soft, about 6 minutes. Add the garlic and stir until tender, 1 to 2 minutes. Place the broth in a small saucepan and bring to a simmer.

2. Raise the heat to medium and add the rice to the skillet. Stir until well coated with olive oil and starting to soften slightly, 2 to 3 minutes. Add 1 cup of the simmering broth. Keep stirring gently until the rice absorbs all the broth. Add the ouzo and stir until absorbed.

3. Add the grated tomato and stir gently until the mixture is dense. Add the remaining broth, 1 cup at a time, stirring until each addition is absorbed, until the rice is creamy but al dente, 25 to 30 minutes.

4. Add the feta and stir until melted and the risotto is creamy and thick. Stir in the oregano and lemon zest, and season to taste with salt and pepper. Remove from the heat and serve immediately.

NOTE: To grate a tomato, halve crosswise and grate the meat side of the tomato using a coarse grater over a strainer set over a bowl. Grate as close to the skin as possible and discard the tomato skin.

Zucchini Pilaf with Almonds

Adapted from Louise Beylerian

TIME: *1 hour*
YIELD: *4 servings*

FOR THE RICE:

½ cup slivered almonds

½ tablespoon butter

½ cup long-grain rice

1 cup vegetable broth

½ teaspoon allspice

½ teaspoon salt

FOR THE ZUCCHINI:

2½ tablespoons olive oil

1 medium onion,
    finely chopped

2 garlic cloves, finely chopped

1 pound zucchini, ends
    trimmed, halved lengthwise
    (or quartered if large) and
    cut into ⅓-inch slices

1 teaspoon ground coriander

1 teaspoon ground cumin

Pinch of cayenne

½ teaspoon salt

2 tablespoons currants
    or dark raisins

The New York interior designer Louise Beylerian left her hometown of Cairo at eighteen to study in the United States. After attending a junior college near Boston, Louise enrolled at Parsons School of Design in Manhattan to be with, and to marry, George Beylerian, the founder of Material ConneXion, a materials consultancy in Manhattan. "I was irresistible," he said, laughing.

He was also hungry, and Louise, then age twenty, couldn't cook.

"My mother had a cook," Mrs. Beylerian explained recently in the kitchen of their country home in Kent, Connecticut. "I tried to recapture the home cooking of my childhood."

So she asked her mother to give her recipes for all the foods they ate, whether they were Egyptian, Armenian, Turkish, or anywhere from the Middle East. She also began to collect cookbooks, and now has hundreds. Among the design world in Manhattan, Mrs. Beylerian is known as a remarkable home cook.

In Egypt, "every lunch and dinner includes rice," she said, as she prepared zucchini pilaf and almonds, a subtly spiced dish that includes tiny amounts of allspice, coriander, cumin, cayenne, and cilantro. To finish the dish, she serves the rice with a thick yogurt-garlic sauce on the side. The garlic is not a mere token addition—though finely minced, it is clearly present and makes yogurt a newly fascinating food.

1. For the rice: Preheat the oven to 350°F. Place the almonds on a baking sheet and bake until lightly toasted, about 10 minutes. Remove and set aside to cool.

3 tablespoons chopped
   cilantro
Freshly ground black pepper

FOR THE YOGURT-GARLIC SAUCE:

1 cup Greek yogurt or strained
   non-Greek plain yogurt
2 garlic cloves, finely chopped
   or pressed through a garlic
   press
1 tablespoon dried
   crushed mint
Pinch of cayenne
Salt and freshly ground
   black pepper

2. In a small pan over medium heat, add the butter and rice. Stir until the rice is lightly toasted, 5 to 8 minutes. Add the vegetable broth, allspice, and salt. Bring to a boil, then reduce the heat to very low so the broth barely simmers; use a heat diffuser if necessary. Cover and cook for 15 minutes.

3. Meanwhile, prepare the zucchini: Place a large sauté pan over medium heat and add the olive oil. Add the onion and cook, stirring, until translucent and lightly browned, about 10 minutes. Add the garlic and cook for 2 minutes. Add the zucchini, coriander, cumin, cayenne, and salt. Cook, stirring, for 5 minutes. Add the rice and currants, and mix well. If the rice looks dry, add 2 tablespoons water. Cover and cook until the zucchini and rice are tender, about 15 minutes. The rice mixture may be uncovered and quickly stirred once or twice, covering it immediately after.

4. For the yogurt-garlic sauce: In a small bowl, combine the yogurt, garlic, mint, and cayenne. Mix well, and season with salt and pepper to taste.

5. When the rice and zucchini are ready, top with the cilantro, toasted almonds, and freshly ground black pepper. Serve immediately, with the yogurt-garlic sauce passed separately.

S

Salade Niçoise

Adapted from Ian Pasquer, Chef, L'Orange Bleue

TIME: 45 minutes
YIELD: 4 servings

FOR THE DRESSING
(MAKES ABOUT 2 1/4 CUPS):

2 tablespoons Dijon mustard

1 tablespoon whole-grain
   mustard

1 1/2 cups extra-virgin
   olive oil

1/3 cup white wine vinegar

1 teaspoon dried thyme

1 teaspoon sea salt

2 teaspoons freshly
   ground black pepper

FOR THE SALAD:

2 to 4 baby Yukon Gold
   potatoes

3 garlic cloves

5 whole black peppercorns

1 bay leaf

Ian Pasquer, a chef at L'Orange Bleue in Manhattan, serves a salade niçoise whose basic ingredients—potatoes, haricots verts, tomatoes, and eggs—are fairly classic, but whose preparation has subtleties that make it especially appealing.

The tiny Yukon Gold potatoes are simmered not in plain water, but with cloves of garlic, whole black peppercorns, a bay leaf, thyme, and salt. Best, the potatoes are served warm. The bed of greens is not just one lettuce, but a mix of romaine, assorted baby lettuces, and arugula. The creamy vinaigrette includes thyme, two mustards—Dijon and whole grain—olive oil, and a splash of water.

"The whole grain mustard makes it more earthy, the thyme gives it a little woody flavor, and the water lightens it," he said of the dressing. (The recipe calls for more dressing than is needed; it will keep refrigerated for two weeks.) He cuts the tomatoes in asymmetrical chunks rather than the expected wedges. "It presents more naturally, since in nature, things are not symmetrical," he added.

Mr. Pasquer grew up in Denver, Colorado, where his parents ran a French language school. Since he was ten, he and his brother, then twelve, and sister, then nine, cooked the family dinner, often French, so that it would be waiting when their parents came home at night.

This salade niçoise is a distillation of every version he has ever made or eaten. It is a complete meal, one that "fills you with a clean taste," he said.

{continued}

1 teaspoon dried thyme

5 tablespoons plus 1 teaspoon
sea salt

2 large eggs

¼ pound haricots verts or
other very small green beans

1½ large or 2 medium
heirloom or other tomatoes

1 romaine lettuce heart,
torn into bite-sized pieces

2 cups arugula

3 cups baby greens

12 niçoise olives, pitted

1. **For the dressing:** In a mixing bowl, combine the Dijon mustard, whole-grain mustard, olive oil, vinegar, thyme, salt, and pepper. Whisk to blend, add ¼ cup water, and whisk again. Cover and refrigerate for up to 2 weeks.

2. **For the salad:** In a medium saucepan, combine the potatoes, garlic, peppercorns, bay leaf, thyme, and 1 tablespoon sea salt. Cover with cold water. Place over high heat to bring to a boil, then reduce the heat to low and simmer until tender, 8 to 10 minutes. Turn off the heat and let stand in the saucepan; do not drain.

3. While the potatoes are simmering, place the eggs and 2 tablespoons salt in a saucepan. Cover with cold water. Place over high heat to bring to a boil, then reduce the heat to low and simmer for 10 minutes. Turn off the heat and let stand in the saucepan; do not drain.

4. In a mixing bowl, combine 3 cups water and 1 cup ice cubes; set aside. In a small saucepan, combine 3 cups water and 2 tablespoons salt. Bring to a boil, add the green beans, and blanch until crisp-tender, 1 to 2 minutes. Drain, rinse under cold water, and transfer to ice water. Allow to sit for 2 minutes, then drain.

5. Cut the tomatoes into 12 irregular chunks and sprinkle with the remaining 1 teaspoon salt. Drain and peel the eggs, and cut each egg lengthwise into quarters. Drain the potatoes and cut into ⅓-inch rounds.

6. In a wide, shallow serving bowl, mix the romaine, arugula, and baby greens. Add 3 tablespoons of the dressing to the greens and toss, adding additional dressing as needed. Arrange the tomatoes, eggs, potatoes, and green beans around the greens, and sprinkle with the olives. Drizzle with some of the remaining dressing. Refrigerate leftover dressing and reserve for another use.

Soybeans with Garlic and Dill

Adapted from Hamid Gharibzade,
Gilaneh, and Maryam Zomorodi, Tehran

TIME: 20 minutes
YIELD: 4 servings

1 tablespoon olive oil

4 tablespoons unsalted butter

1 large onion, thinly sliced

5 garlic cloves, minced

1/4 teaspoon salt, or to taste

1/2 teaspoon freshly ground
   black pepper, or to taste

1 teaspoon turmeric

4 tablespoons minced
   fresh dill, or 2 tablespoons
   dried dill

1 1/2 cups fresh or frozen
   shelled edamame

Cooked rice, for serving
   (optional)

I first ate a version of this wonderful dish at Gilaneh restaurant in Tehran on a late spring day at the end of May 2009, weeks before Iran's presidential election and the disputed voting results that brought turmoil to the city.

On that day, nothing could have been more peaceful than lunch by an open window two stories above a bustling street: lamb kebabs, chicken in a tangy pomegranate sauce, and a dish of beans in a buttery sauce tinted pale yellow from turmeric and flecked with garlic and dill. The restaurant used fava beans. The chef, Hamid Gharibzade, explained how he made the dish, called *baqala qataq*.

Later on, Maryam Zomorodi, a caterer I had met, cooked it in a friend's home kitchen.

"In northern Iran, it is a common dish, a daily dish, eaten with eggs and rice," Ms. Zomorodi said. She cooked it in a blue-green clay pot, called a *gamaj*, and swore that the dish was far tastier when cooked that way than in a metal pot. Tweaking the restaurant's recipe, Ms. Zomorodi sautéed a mound of thinly sliced onions as the beans were cooking.

Back home in New York, I wanted to adapt the quick-cooking recipe, which takes about twenty-five minutes, for year-round preparation. Instead of using fava beans, which are both seasonal and tiresome to peel, I used frozen shelled soybeans (edamame). The simple dish, whose secret lies partly in the lavish amount of butter, merrily survived the change.

{continued}

1. Fill a kettle with 3 cups water and bring to a boil. Meanwhile, place a medium saucepan over medium-low heat, add the olive oil and butter, and heat until bubbling. Add the onion and sauté until soft, about 8 minutes.

2. Add the garlic and sauté until pale gold, about 5 minutes. Add the salt, pepper, turmeric, and dill. Stir for 1 minute. Add the edamame and enough boiling water to barely cover the beans.

3. Simmer until the beans are just tender, 2 to 3 minutes. Adjust the salt and pepper to taste. Serve hot, using a slotted spoon to drain any excess liquid. If desired, serve with rice.

Spinach Saag with Spiced Potato Balls

Adapted from Eric McCarthy, Executive Chef, Tamarind Tribeca

TIME: 35 minutes
YIELD: 4 servings

2 pounds large-leaf spinach

1/4 cup olive oil

1 cup finely chopped onion

1 tablespoon finely chopped garlic

1 tablespoon finely chopped fresh ginger

3 to 4 Thai bird chiles, each about 1 1/2 inches long, seeded and finely chopped

1 pound baby spinach

1 teaspoon turmeric

Salt

1/4 cup dried fenugreek leaves (*kasuri methi*)

1 tablespoon butter

1/4 teaspoon freshly grated nutmeg

1/2 cup heavy cream (optional)

Spiced Potato Balls (recipe follows)

Julia Moskin, a reporter in the Dining Section of the *New York Times*, walked by my desk with a glint in her eye and said, "I have a dish for you!"

I perked up. Her palate is flawless.

"Saag with some kind of fried, spiced potato balls on top—like Tater Tots," she said.

It was the potato balls that had enchanted her.

The dish was Subz Saag at Tamarind Tribeca in Manhattan. The saag was a mix of mustard greens, broccoli rabe, and corn, but the topping consisted of the mysterious potato balls. Called *alu kofta*, the golden, deep-fried mashed potato balls are 1 1/2 inches in diameter, and gently spiced with garlic, ginger, chile, turmeric, and lemon juice. They are addictive.

Eric McCarthy, the executive chef at Tamarind Tribeca, simplified the dish a bit.

When he makes spinach saag (*saag* means "greens" and *palak* means "spinach") he uses two kinds of spinach. He blanches regular, large-leafed spinach, then drains and chops it. He leaves the baby spinach whole, adds it toward the end to give a little more texture to the beautifully spiced dish, and then serves it topped with India's answer to Tater Tots. Or perhaps Tater Tots is America's answer to *alu kofta*.

{continued}

1. Prepare a large bowl of ice water and set aside. Place a large pot of water over high heat and bring to a boil. Add the large-leaf spinach, and blanch until bright green and tender, 1 to 2 minutes. Drain, immediately plunge into ice water until cooled, and drain again. Squeeze out the excess moisture, chop finely, and set aside.

2. In a large sauté pan over medium heat, heat the olive oil until shimmering. Add the onion, and cook until soft and golden, 7 to 8 minutes. Add the garlic, ginger, and chiles, and sauté until the garlic and ginger are light brown, 2 to 3 minutes. Add the baby spinach and cook 1 minute. Add the turmeric and sauté 2 to 3 minutes.

3. Add the blanched chopped spinach. Season with salt to taste. Cook 5 to 10 minutes, stirring often. Add the fenugreek, butter, nutmeg, and, heavy cream, if desired. Simmer 5 minutes more, stirring occasionally. If necessary, lower the heat to medium-low. Serve hot, topped with Spiced Potato Balls, if desired.

Spiced Potato Balls (*Alu Kofta*)

TIME: 40 minutes
YIELD: 16 small potato balls
(4 servings)

2 medium potatoes, peeled
(to yield 2 cups cooked
and mashed)
1 tablespoon vegetable oil,
plus 3 cups or as needed
for deep-frying

1. Place the potatoes in a medium saucepan and add cold water to cover by an inch. Bring to a boil, lower the heat, and simmer until the potatoes are fork-tender, about 15 minutes. Drain and mash with a fork.

2. In a large skillet over medium heat, combine 1 tablespoon oil, the ginger, garlic, chile, and chile flakes. Sauté until the ginger and garlic are golden brown. Add the mashed potatoes, turmeric, cornstarch, lemon juice, and cilantro, if using. Reduce the heat to low and cook for 5 minutes, stirring often. Season with salt to taste.

1 teaspoon finely chopped
   ginger
1 teaspoon finely chopped
   garlic
1 teaspoon finely chopped
   seeded Thai bird chile
   (optional)
¼ teaspoon chile flakes
½ teaspoon turmeric
3 tablespoons cornstarch
1 tablespoon lemon juice
½ cup chopped cilantro
   (optional)
Salt

3. Remove the potatoes from the heat and allow to cool to room temperature. Meanwhile, heat the 3 cups vegetable oil in a deep fryer or wok to 350°F.

4. Make 16 round balls, about 1½ inches in diameter, from the potato mixture. Working in batches if necessary, fry the balls until golden brown, about 6 to 8 minutes. Drain on paper towels and serve hot.

T

Tempura (Vegan)

Adapted from Masato Nishihara, Executive Chef, Kajitsu

TIME: *30 minutes,*
  plus 3 hours' soaking
YIELD: *2 servings*

FOR THE DIPPING SAUCE:

1/2 ounce dried kelp kombu

1 dried shiitake mushroom,
  stem removed

1 tablespoon mirin
  (available in Asian markets
  and some supermarkets)

1 tablespoon light soy sauce

1 tablespoon peeled grated
  daikon

1/2 teaspoon peeled grated
  ginger

FOR THE TEMPURA:

Vegetable oil, for frying

1 cup plus 2 tablespoons cake
  flour, plus 1/2 cup or as
  needed for dipping

4 to 5 1/3-inch-thick slices
  zucchini, ends trimmed

Masato Nishihara, the executive chef of Kajitsu, an elegant vegan Japanese restaurant in the East Village in Manhattan, created a vegan vegetable tempura, one without eggs in the batter. "He believes that tempura batter originally was just flour and water, and that when you go back in history, at some point someone added eggs," said Chiaki Takada, who interpreted for Mr. Nishihara. The chef said that the differences between the two tempuras—one with eggs, the other without—are not big.

"With a batter with eggs, the fried coating becomes fluffy, the coating gets a rich flavor, and the color looks bright yellow," Ms. Takada said. "With a batter without eggs, the fried coating becomes crisp and the taste of the ingredient inside stands out more."

What makes a successful tempura, however, has little to do with the egg question. "It's more about how you cut the ingredient, the thickness of the batter, and the oil temperature," Ms. Takada said.

1. For the dipping sauce: Combine the kelp and shiitake mushroom in a small bowl. Add 1 cup cold water and allow to soak for 3 hours. Strain and set the clear, amber liquid aside; discard the kelp and mushroom. In a small pot oven medium heat, combine the mirin and soy sauce and bring to a boil. Add 1/2 cup of the soaking liquid from the kelp and mushroom. Remove from heat and put aside. In a separate bowl, mix the daikon and ginger; set aside.

{continued}

4 to 5 ⅓-inch-thick slices
slender Asian eggplant,
ends trimmed

4 to 5 ¼-inch-thick slices
yam, peeled or unpeeled,
ends trimmed

2. For the tempura: Pour oil into a large wok or pot so that the oil is 2 inches deep. Heat over medium-high heat until the oil is 350°F. Set aside a baking sheet with a rack lined with paper towels, and a small, long-handled, fine-meshed strainer for removing excess fried batter.

3. Pour 1 cup ice-cold water into a medium bowl. Add 1 cup plus 2 tablespoons cake flour and whisk to blend. Place about ½ cup cake flour into another bowl. Dip each slice of vegetable into the dry flour, shake off the excess, and then dip each slice into the batter.

4. Fry the vegetables in batches to be sure they are not crowded. Place 4 to 6 vegetable pieces in the oil and fry, turning once or twice, until golden and crisp, 2 to 2½ minutes. Using the long-handled strainer, remove excess bits of fried batter to keep the oil clean. Transfer the vegetables to the baking sheet to drain. Continue until all the vegetables are fried.

5. To serve, place a paper napkin in the center of a platter and arrange the vegetables on the platter. Pour off the excess moisture from the grated daikon and grated ginger. Place the daikon and ginger mixture in the center of the dipping sauce, arranged as a little pointed mound. Serve the tempura with the dipping sauce.

General Tso's Tofu Sub

Adapted from Tyler Kord, Chef-Owner, No. 7 Sub and No. 7

TIME: *1 hour and 15 minutes*
YIELD: *2 to 4 servings*

FOR THE GENERAL TSO SAUCE:

1 small chunk ginger, 1½ inches long, peeled and roughly chopped

1 garlic clove, roughly chopped

¼ cup soy sauce

2 tablespoons sweet soy sauce

2 tablespoons white vinegar

2 tablespoons mirin

½ teaspoon sesame oil

1½ small red dry Chinese chiles

½ teaspoon salt

½ teaspoon sugar

½ teaspoon xanthan gum (optional)

FOR THE PICKLES:

2 garlic cloves, roughly chopped

1 small chunk ginger, 1 inch long, peeled and sliced against the grain

Half a shallot, roughly chopped

¼ teaspoon sesame oil

Tyler Kord, the chef-owner of No. 7 Sub in Manhattan and No. 7 in Fort Greene, Brooklyn, has made the submarine a thing of juiciness, beauty, and exoticism. "I like soft bread and fancy ingredients inside," said Mr. Kord, who worked at a Subway when he was sixteen, growing up in Ithaca, New York, and eventually became sous-chef at Jean-Georges Vongerichten's Perry Street restaurant in New York.

Take General Tso's Tofu Sub, a brilliant study of layered textures and flavors. The centerpiece is a deep-fried panko-crusted rectangle of firm tofu, golden and crusty outside and creamy inside. Mr. Kord layers the tofu between edamame puree, homemade pickled cucumbers, and a piquant sauce named after General Tso that includes ginger, garlic, soy sauce, vinegar, sesame oil, sugar, and chiles.

The blender does the work in three quick steps.

The result is startling. It is what Mr. Kord wants it to be: crunchy, creamy, salty, sweet, and sour, all in one bite. The sandwich is the creation of Mr. Kord and his chef de cuisine, Gabriel Llanos.

And the rolls? They are soft and springy buns, "easy to sink your teeth into," Mr. Kord said, and are from a bakery in Crown Heights, Brooklyn, owned by Mr. Kord and his partners.

1. For the General Tso sauce: In a blender, combine the ginger, garlic, soy sauce, sweet soy sauce, vinegar, mirin, and sesame oil. Add chiles,

{continued}

½ teaspoon sugar

1½ teaspoons salt

1 small red dry Chinese chile, seeded

½ cup white wine vinegar

1 scallion, in 3-inch lengths, sliced vertically into chiffonade

1½ cucumbers, peeled, seeded, and sliced crosswise ⅛ inch thick

FOR THE EDAMAME PUREE:

¾ cup frozen shelled edamame, thawed

FOR THE TOFU:

Vegetable oil, for deep-frying

¼ cup salt

1½ teaspoons sugar

¼ teaspoon paprika

¼ teaspoon garlic powder

¼ teaspoon onion powder

8 ounces firm tofu, drained and cut into 4 slices

3 large egg whites

3 tablespoons cornstarch

½ cup panko bread crumbs

FOR ASSEMBLY:

2 submarine sandwich rolls

Mayonnaise

Sesame seeds

salt, sugar, and xanthan gum, if using. Process until smooth. Transfer to a small bowl and set aside.

2. For the pickles: In a clean blender, combine the garlic, ginger, shallot, sesame oil, sugar, salt, and chile. Blend until slightly smooth but still mostly chunky. Transfer to a medium bowl, and add the vinegar, scallion, and cucumbers. Mix and set aside.

3. For the edamame puree: In a clean blender, puree the edamame and add just enough water to make a smooth paste. Transfer to a small bowl and set aside.

4. For the tofu: In a deep fryer, preheat the vegetable oil to 350°F. Meanwhile, in a small bowl, mix together the salt, sugar, paprika, garlic powder, and onion powder. Place the tofu on a plate and use 1 tablespoon of the salt mixture to lightly sprinkle both sides of the tofu. Reserve the rest of the salt mixture for another use.

5. In a medium bowl, whisk together the egg whites and cornstarch until blended and smooth. Place the panko in a shallow bowl. Dip the seasoned tofu slices into the egg white batter, gently shake off the excess batter, and dip in the panko, covering the tofu thoroughly. Deep-fry in the oil until deep golden brown, about 4 minutes. Remove and drain.

6. For assembly: Cut the rolls open lengthwise. Spread one side of each with the edamame puree and the other side with mayonnaise. Quickly dip both sides of the fried tofu in the General Tso sauce, and place 2 slices of tofu, end to end, on one side of each roll. Top the tofu with drained pickled cucumbers, garnish with a sprinkle of sesame seeds, and finish by topping with the other side of the roll. Cut in half and serve immediately.

Ma Po Tofu (Vegan)

Adapted from Susur Lee, Executive Chef, Shang and Lee

TIME: *1 hour*
YIELD: *2 servings*

2 tablespoons olive oil

½ teaspoon ground Sichuan pepper, plus additional as needed

1 tablespoon finely chopped garlic

2 tablespoons vegetarian oyster sauce

1 tablespoon hot bean paste (also known as spiced broad bean sauce), or as needed

1 tablespoon soy sauce

1 teaspoon sugar

1 teaspoon chile (hot) sesame oil, plus additional for drizzling

Half a Thai bird chile, seeded and minced

Freshly ground white pepper

"Ma Po Tofu is supposed to bring sweat to your face and numbness to your mouth," said Susur Lee, the executive chef of Shang in Manhattan and Lee in Toronto. His famous dish of silken tofu is made fiery with hot bean paste, Thai bird chiles, and ground Sichuan pepper, and rounded out with soy sauce, vegetarian oyster sauce, and garlic. It is best eaten over soothing, bland rice.

When I ate my first three bites of Ma Po Tofu in the dining room at Shang, tiny beads of perspiration popped up on my forehead. My eyes began to tear. My nose began to run. I blinked back tears and said to Mr. Lee: "Where's the ladies' room? I need tissues!" He pointed. I ran.

Five minutes later, I returned to the table. Mr. Lee said, grinning, "That's the perfect reaction!"

As I picked up my chopsticks again, I tripled the amount of rice for every bite of Ma Po tofu, and ate it gingerly and defensively. Despite the fieriness, it was delicious.

Mr. Lee, who has been cooking since he was fourteen when he started working at the Peninsula Hotel in Hong Kong, is impervious to the spiciness of the Ma Po tofu. As he ate, his unfurrowed brow remained perfectly dry.

He has adjusted the recipe here so that it does not bring sweat to the brow and tears to the eyes. For greater spice, you may increase the amounts of Sichuan pepper, hot bean sauce, chile sesame oil, and Thai bird chile, but only in very small increments. Proceed with caution—taste as you season.

{continued}

2 teaspoons black Chinese
vinegar or balsamic
vinegar

One 16-ounce package silken
tofu, drained and cut in
3/4-inch cubes

1/4 cup minced Chinese
preserved vegetable
(mustard green root)
(see Note)

2 teaspoons cornstarch

1 tablespoon julienned ginger,
placed in a bowl of cold
water

12 whole coriander leaves, plus
stems, minced

1 tablespoon minced red bell
pepper

Cooked rice, for serving
(optional)

1. In a wok over medium heat, heat the olive oil until shimmering. Add 1/2 teaspoon Sichuan pepper and stir rapidly for 30 seconds. Add the garlic and stir rapidly for 30 seconds. Remove the wok from the heat, and add the oyster sauce, 1 cup water, hot bean paste, soy sauce, sugar, 1 teaspoon chile sesame oil, the Thai chile, a pinch of white pepper, the vinegar, and tofu.

2. Place the wok over high heat and cook, stirring, until bubbling, 3 to 5 minutes. Add the preserved vegetable. As it begins to heat up, adjust the hot bean paste as desired, a teaspoon at a time, up to 3 teaspoons. (This amount will make it tear-inducing hot, the fieriness that Susur Lee likes.) The sauce will begin to thicken just slightly.

3. In a small bowl, mix the cornstarch with 1/4 cup cold water. Pour into the wok, stirring very gently, so as not to break up the tofu. Simmer until the sauce is glossy, 30 seconds to 1 minute.

4. Transfer to a medium serving bowl, and garnish with the drained julienned ginger, coriander leaves and stems, a drizzle of sesame oil, red bell pepper, and, if desired, a sprinkle of Sichuan pepper. If desired, serve with rice.

NOTE: Chinese preserved mustard roots, also known as Chinese preserved vegetable, are available vacuum packed, canned, or in open bins, sometimes dusted with chili powder, in many Asian stores. If it comes flecked with chili powder, rinse it off and pat dry.

Moroccan Stuffed Tomatoes (Vegan)

Adapted from Anissa Helou

TIME: *1 hour and 15 minutes*
YIELD: *2 to 3 servings*

3 tablespoons extra-virgin
   olive oil, plus additional for
   brushing baking dish

6 medium vine-ripe tomatoes,
   tops sliced off and seeds
   removed

Sea salt

1 medium onion, very thinly
   sliced

2 garlic cloves, minced

1 pound firm medium zucchini,
   trimmed and grated

3 tablespoons finely chopped
   cilantro

1/3 teaspoon chile flakes,
   or to taste

2 tablespoons toasted shelled
   pistachios, plus 2 teaspoons
   for garnish

Imagine a juicy red tomato stuffed with sautéed slivers of green zucchini, onion, garlic, cilantro, and pistachios, and then garnished with yet more pistachios.

Anissa Helou, the Lebanese cookbook author and food consultant based in London, first ate this stuffed tomato in Morocco many years ago. She has been making it ever since.

"I like the contrast between the green stuffing and the red tomatoes, the freshness of the vegetable stuffing with the added crunch of the toasted peeled pistachios, and the way the tomatoes caramelize while baking in the oven," she said. "Not to mention that it is supremely healthy."

1. Preheat the oven to 350°F. Brush a small baking dish, large enough to hold the tomatoes snugly, with a little olive oil. Arrange the tomatoes in the dish, cut-side up, and sprinkle lightly with salt.

2. Place a large frying pan over medium-high heat and add 3 tablespoons olive oil. Heat until shimmering. Add the onion and sauté until golden and translucent, about 5 minutes. Add the garlic and zucchini, and sauté until the zucchini is just starting to soften, about 2 minutes.

{continued}

3. Remove the pan from the heat, and add the cilantro, chile flakes, and 2 tablespoons pistachios. Season with salt to taste, mixing well. Divide the filling equally among the tomatoes, mounding the tops.

4. Bake for 45 minutes, or until the vegetables are cooked as desired. Garnish with the remaining 2 teaspoons pistachios. Serve warm or at room temperature.

Roasted Tomato and Eggplant Tartine

Adapted from Marc Murphy,
Executive Chef-Owner, Landmarc and Ditch Plains

TIME: 40 minutes
YIELD: 4 servings

FOR THE TOMATOES:

1 very large or 2 medium
   beefsteak tomatoes,
   thinly sliced
1 tablespoon extra-virgin
   olive oil
3 garlic cloves, chopped
1 tablespoon chopped fresh
   thyme

FOR THE TAPENADE:

1/2 cup pitted kalamata olives
2 tablespoons drained capers
1/4 cup extra-virgin olive oil

FOR ASSEMBLY:

3/4 pound eggplant, sliced
   lengthwise into 4 slices,
   each about 1/3 inch thick

"We're actively trying to please vegetarians," said Marc Murphy, the executive chef and owner of the Landmarc and Ditch Plains restaurants.

Three years ago he introduced a roasted tomato and eggplant tartine at the two Landmarc locations. It's an open-faced sandwich layered with goat cheese, grilled eggplant, tapenade, and roasted tomatoes. The tartine, sprinkled with grated Pecorino Romano cheese, captures the flavors of his childhood. Mr. Murphy was born in Milan to a French mother and an American father. "I grew up with these flavors of France and Italy."

The tartine is as rich in flavor as it is easy to make. "Sorry it's so boring and simple," said Mr. Murphy, who suggests serving it with a salad.

1. For the tomatoes: Preheat the oven to 300°F. In a wide, shallow bowl, toss the tomato slices with the olive oil, garlic, and thyme. Spread on a baking sheet. Roast 20 minutes. Remove from the heat and set aside.

2. For the tapenade: Place the olives and capers in a blender or food processor and chop coarsely. With the motor running, slowly drizzle in the olive oil. Puree until smooth; set aside.

{continued}

3 tablespoons olive oil

Salt and freshly ground
  black pepper

½ cup fresh soft goat cheese

Four ½-inch slices
  country bread

¼ cup grated Pecorino
  Romano cheese

3. For assembly: Prepare a grill for cooking or heat a ridged grill pan over moderately high heat. Brush both sides of the eggplant slices with olive oil, and season with salt and pepper to taste. Grill, turning as necessary, until slightly charred and soft, about 3 to 4 minutes a side.

4. Preheat a broiler. Spread a thin layer of goat cheese on each slice of bread. Top each with an equal portion of eggplant, tapenade, and roasted tomatoes. Sprinkle with the grated cheese. Broil until the cheese is melted and the tartine is piping hot, about 5 minutes.

Summer Vegetables in Saffron Broth with Ricotta and Toasted Baguette

Adapted from Christopher Lee

TIME: 35 minutes
YIELD: 4 servings

FOR THE VEGETABLES AND BROTH:

¼ cup extra-virgin olive oil

12 whole peeled baby carrots, preferably with an inch of green tops left on

2 fennel bulbs, trimmed of green tops, quartered

2 shallots or 1 sweet onion, thinly sliced

8 scallions, roots trimmed, cut into thirds

8 fingerling potatoes, cut into thirds

1 cup fresh corn kernels

1 cup white wine

Large pinch of saffron

Small pinch of cayenne

2 bay leaves

3 sprigs thyme

In midsummer 2007, Christopher Lee found himself at a farm stand in Mattituck, on Long Island, New York.

"I bought English peas, tomatoes, corn, summer squash, onion, garlic, a bunch of herbs, red bell peppers," said Mr. Lee, who was the executive chef at Gilt at the time. "Anything I saw, I basically grabbed. Then I put it together."

He concocted a fresh summer soup and heightened the flavors with a large pinch of saffron.

"It's an intense flavor layering: floral with a nutty sensation," he said. "I threw whatever I could find into the soup, and I served it with a baguette."

Mr. Lee was, until December 2010, the chef at Aureole, which moved from the Upper East Side to the Bryant Park area. For diners who were vegetarian, he asked the waiters to recommend dishes like this saffron broth. The vegetables vary by season. To the baguette he added ricotta "for a little more substance."

As if all those vegetables weren't enough.

1. For the vegetables and broth: Place a 6-quart saucepan over high heat. When the pan is hot, add the olive oil, carrots, fennel, shallots or sweet onion, scallions, potatoes, and corn. Reduce the heat to medium-low. Sauté 2 minutes, then add 4 cups water, the wine, saffron, cayenne, bay leaves, and thyme.

{continued}

1 cup haricots verts
  or green beans
1 cup fresh or frozen green
  peas
1 pint cherry tomatoes,
  each halved
3 tablespoons unsalted butter
3 sprigs tarragon
Salt and freshly ground black
  pepper

FOR THE BAGUETTE
AND RICOTTA:

Four 1/2-inch-thick baguette
  slices
1/4 pound fresh ricotta

2. Bring to a simmer and cook until the carrots and potatoes are just tender, about 15 minutes. Add the haricots verts or green beans, peas, tomatoes, butter, and tarragon. Season to taste with salt and pepper. Remove and discard the bay leaves and thyme sprigs. Simmer for another 5 minutes before serving, or remove from the heat for up to 20 minutes, then reheat.

3. For the baguette and ricotta: Grill or toast the baguette slices, then spread each with ricotta.

4. To serve: Divide the vegetables and broth equally among four bowls. Garnish each with a slice of baguette and ricotta.

W

Grilled Watermelon and Tomato Salad (Vegan)

Adapted from Daniel Humm, Executive Chef, Eleven Madison Park

TIME: *15 minutes, plus preheating charcoal grill or grill pan*
YIELD: *4 appetizer servings*

Four ¾-inch-thick seedless watermelon slices, as needed

4 ripe heirloom tomatoes, mixed colors, cut into batons with an apple corer or sliced into wedges

4 tablespoons extra-virgin olive oil

Kosher salt and freshly ground black pepper

1 tablespoon fresh lemon juice

4 teaspoons aged balsamic vinegar

8 small fresh opal basil leaves

8 small fresh green basil leaves

Maldon sea salt, for garnish

In 2004, Daniel Humm, now the executive chef at Eleven Madison Park, was traveling in Barcelona, Spain, and discovered cooks grilling slices of melon and serving them at a tapas bar. They were juicy and smoky but not cooked. "I had the idea in my head for several years," he said.

In May 2010, he introduced to the menu of his Manhattan restaurant a salad of grilled watermelon and heirloom tomatoes, lightly dressed with olive oil and aged balsamic vinegar and garnished with tiny leaves of fresh opal basil and fresh green basil.

The salad contrasts the sweetness of the melon with the gentle acidity of the tomatoes. The visual beauty of the salad lies in the different colored tomatoes—red, green, orange, yellow. But if you have only red ones, the salad will still be delicious. The more aged the balsamic, the more intense the flavor.

He heats the grill to very hot. "You don't want the grill to be just warm, and you don't want the watermelon cooked," he said. "You're looking for coloring and a smoky smell." The melon sits on the grill for about 2 minutes.

Although Mr. Humm uses an apple corer to make the batons of tomatoes, he said that the home cook can simply cut the tomatoes into wedges.

{continued}

1. Outdoors, prepare a charcoal grill for direct grilling over high heat. Indoors, place a grill pan over high heat until very hot.

2. Using a 3½-inch cookie cutter, cut the watermelon flesh into 4 rounds. Place on the grill grates or in the grill pan directly over the heat. Grill on one side only, until grill marked and the melon emits a slightly smoky aroma, about 2 minutes. Transfer the rounds, grill marked–sides up, to a platter.

3. Place the tomato batons or wedges in a large bowl and toss gently with 2 tablespoons olive oil. Season to taste with kosher salt, pepper, and lemon juice.

4. Place a watermelon round, grill marked–side up, in the center of each of four appetizer plates. Top each with an equal portion of tomatoes. Drizzle each salad with ½ tablespoon of the remaining olive oil and top each with 1 teaspoon balsamic vinegar. Garnish with opal basil, green basil, and a few grains of Maldon salt, and serve.

Green Wheat and Roasted Vegetables with Herb Salad (Vegan)

Adapted from Shanna Pacifico, Back Forty

TIME: 45 minutes
YIELD: 4 servings

FOR THE GREEN WHEAT:

¼ cup extra-virgin olive oil

1 cup mixed diced (⅓-inch)
  carrot, onion, and celery

1 bay leaf

3 cups green wheat
  (labeled as *frik*—see Note)

5½ cups vegetable broth
  or water

Salt and freshly ground
  black pepper

4 cups spinach leaves

**FOR THE ROASTED VEGETABLES
(CHOOSE 4 OR 5 FROM LIST
BELOW):**

1 bunch asparagus, trimmed of
  coarse bottom ends

1 cup baby turnips, halved

Roasted green wheat has many aliases: *frik, freek, frieka, freekeh,* and *firik,* among them. They are all variations of an Arabic word.

For American cooks unfamiliar with the word and the grain, here is a primer from Peter Hoffman, the owner of Savoy and Back Forty in Manhattan.

"It's wheat that's picked when it's still green and hasn't dried at all on the stalk," he said.

To preserve the wheat and cook out some of its moisture, it is roasted over a wood fire, he said, "so it picks up a little bit of smoke as it's drying and curing."

In Lebanon and Syria, the grain is often used in pilafs.

Paula Wolfert, the cookbook author, ate it in Aleppo, Syria, topped with a sauce of ground lamb and flecked with tiny peas and chopped pistachios.

Shanna Pacifico learned about *frik* two years ago when she was a sous-chef at Savoy. Mr. Hoffman had used the grain on his menus and told her about it. She found a package of *frik* at Kalustyan's, an Indian food store on lower Lexington Avenue, and started experimenting.

When Mr. Hoffman opened Back Forty in the East Village, he asked Ms. Pacifico to be chef de cuisine there. She put *frik* on her menu right away.

"I wanted to have a nice vegetarian option dish that had wheat, that was hearty and would be filling and delicious," she said. "I thought it would be good with roasted vegetables."

{continued}

1 cup peeled cipolline onions
    or spring onions, halved if
    larger than a quarter
1 cup baby carrots, trimmed
1 cup fennel bulb, thinly sliced
    with core still attached
1 cup yellow or green wax
    beans, trimmed
1 cup morel or shiitake
    mushrooms, cleaned and
    trimmed of stems
1 bunch spring garlic or ¼ cup
    small (or halved if large)
    garlic cloves
5 sprigs thyme
Extra-virgin olive oil

FOR THE HERB SALAD:

¼ cup parsley leaves
¼ cup basil leaves
¼ cup whole mint leaves
Juice and finely grated zest of
    1 lemon
¼ cup pitted kalamata or
    other briny black olives,
    halved lengthwise
Extra-virgin olive oil
Salt and freshly ground
    black pepper

Substituting a different grain, like bulgur or brown rice, for the *frik* in this recipe will work.

"But the thing about frik is its nice, smoky flavor," Ms. Pacifico said. "It adds more oomph to the dish."

1. For the green wheat: Place a medium saucepan over medium heat, and add the olive oil, diced vegetables, and bay leaf. Stir, cover, and cook, stirring occasionally, until tender, about 5 minutes. Add the green wheat and cook, uncovered, stirring, until lightly browned, 3 to 5 minutes. Add the broth or water, and season to taste with salt and pepper. Cover and reduce the heat to low. Simmer, stirring every 5 minutes, for 30 minutes. Meanwhile, prepare the roasted vegetables and herb salad.

2. For roasted vegetables: Preheat the oven to 400°F. Spread the vegetables, mushrooms, garlic, and thyme in a roasting pan. Lightly coat with the olive oil and season liberally with salt and pepper. Roast until just tender (be careful not to overcook), about 20 minutes.

3. For the herb salad: In a medium bowl, combine the parsley, basil, mint, lemon juice and zest, and olives. Add olive oil to taste, and season with salt and pepper.

4. To serve: When the *frik* is cooked, mix in the spinach just before serving, and adjust the salt and pepper to taste. Place a serving of green wheat in the center of each of four plates, and arrange the roasted vegetables on top as desired. Garnish each plate with herb salad and serve immediately.

NOTE: *Frik* is sold at Kalustyan's, 123 Lexington Avenue (28th Street), (800) 352-3451, and at kalustyans.com. It is also available at S.O.S. Chefs, 104 Avenue B (Seventh Street), (212) 505-5813.

Y

Yogurt Soup

Adapted from Gary MacGurn,
Executive Chef and an Owner, Hampton Chutney Co.

TIME: *1 hour*
YIELD: *6 servings*

2 cups diced (³/₄-inch) peeled
    butternut squash

1 teaspoon salt

¼ teaspoon black pepper, or
    to taste

4 tablespoons olive oil

¼ cup chickpea flour

4 garlic cloves, peeled and
    smashed

3 thin slices peeled fresh
    ginger

1 teaspoon finely chopped
    jalapeño pepper

4 cups whole milk plain yogurt

½ teaspoon black mustard
    seeds

In the '70s, and again in the '80s, Gary MacGurn lived in India for five years altogether. While there, he learned to make dosas, chutneys, and khadi, a yogurt soup. He has since become the executive chef and an owner of Hampton Chutney in Amagansett and Manhattan, where his dosas are paper thin, and his khadi is a creamy ivory soup, studded with cubes of roasted butternut squash and flecks of cilantro.

It is the subtle use of spices, both in the yogurt base and in the sautéing of the onions, that gives the soup character. He adds a blended paste of chickpea flour (for thickening), garlic, ginger, and jalapeño pepper to the base. He sautés the onion with black mustard seeds, cumin, and fresh curry leaves.

In India, he said, the soup is often served with pakoras, little fried dumplings, but not at Hampton Chutney. "We don't normally, or hardly ever, deep-fry at Hampton Chutney," he said. "We try to keep it a little healthier and a little less oily."

The soup is one of his staples. "I've been making it, oh gosh, a good thirty years," he said.

{continued}

1 teaspoon ground cumin

8 fresh curry leaves

1 large onion, thinly sliced

⅓ cup brown sugar

¼ cup chopped cilantro,
   or to taste

1. Preheat the oven to 350°F. In a roasting pan, toss together the squash, salt, pepper, and 2 tablespoons olive oil. Roast, uncovered, until tender and golden brown, about 30 minutes.

2. In a blender, combine the chickpea flour, garlic, ginger, jalapeño, and ½ cup water. Blend until smooth. Transfer to a stockpot and add 3½ cups water and the yogurt. Place over high heat and stir until smooth and creamy. Bring to a boil, then remove from the heat.

3. In a sauté pan over medium heat, heat the remaining 2 tablespoons olive oil until shimmering. Add the mustard seeds; they will pop. When the popping begins to subside, stir in the cumin and curry leaves. When the cumin turns golden brown, add the onion and cook until translucent.

4. Add the onion mixture, roasted squash, and brown sugar to the stockpot. Season with salt to taste. Return to medium heat until steaming. To serve, ladle into bowls and garnish with the cilantro.

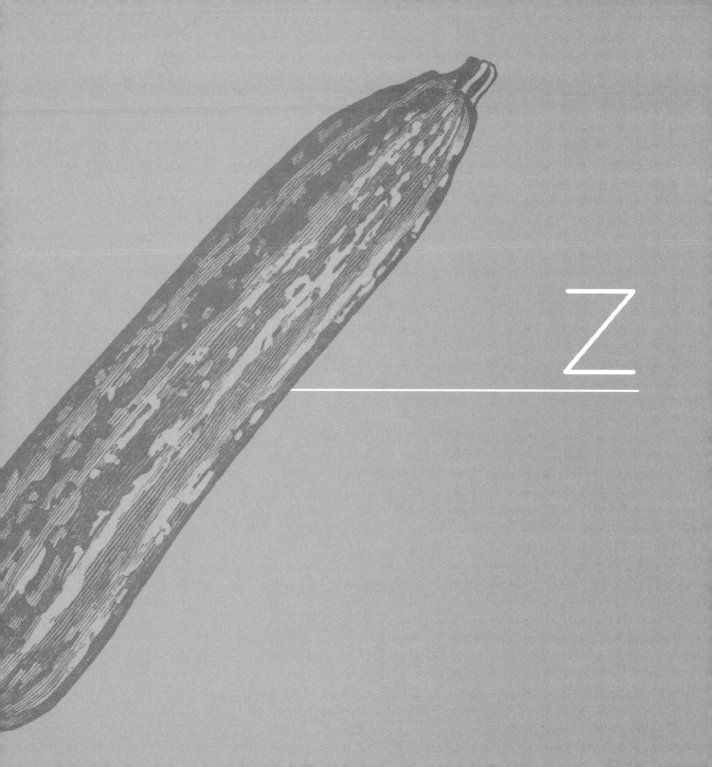

Z

Zucchini and Cheese Pie

Adapted from Louise Beylerian

TIME: 1 hour and 15 minutes
YIELD: 4 to 6 servings

Nonstick cooking spray

2 tablespoons extra-virgin
olive oil

1½ pounds zucchini, trimmed
and cut crosswise into
⅛-inch slices

Salt and freshly ground
black pepper

2 tablespoons finely chopped
fresh dill

1 cup grated Monterey Jack
cheese

½ cup crumbled feta cheese

2 tablespoons butter

2 tablespoons flour

1½ cups milk

1 large egg, beaten

¼ teaspoon grated nutmeg

Louise Beylerian, a former interior designer, who is half Armenian and half German, grew up mostly in Cairo. At age eighteen she came to the United States. In Cairo, the family cook made this addictive cheese and zucchini pie (often with less cheese and more lamb), and the family would eat it on Sunday nights, accompanied by a salad. It is so delicious that it can be eaten for dinner and then again for breakfast the next day.

It is a fusion dish, a result of Egypt being first a French colony, then later a British colony. "The French and English influences were always there, especially in the cooking of the upper classes," Ms. Beylerian said. "Therefore, the béchamel, which is not typically Egyptian, became an adaptation."

1. Preheat the oven to 375°F. Spray a deep 9-inch pie dish with cooking spray; set aside.

2. Place a large skillet over medium-high heat, add the olive oil, and heat until shimmering. Place a single layer of zucchini in the skillet. Cook until lightly browned on one side, 3 to 4 minutes. Turn the zucchini over and cook until lightly browned on the other side, another 3 to 4 minutes. Season lightly with salt and pepper. Remove and place on paper towels. Repeat with the remaining zucchini.

{continued}

3. Arrange one layer of zucchini in the pie dish. Sprinkle with 1 table-spoon dill, and top with the Monterey Jack and feta. Add a second layer of zucchini and remaining tablespoon of dill.

4. In a small pan over medium heat, melt the butter until bubbling. Add the flour and whisk over medium heat for 6 to 8 minutes. Add the milk, raise the heat to medium-high, and whisk until the sauce has thickened considerably, 3 to 5 minutes. Remove from the heat and let cool for 3 minutes. Whisk the beaten egg into the sauce. Add the nut-meg, and season with salt and pepper to taste. Pour over the zucchini mixture. Bake until firm and lightly browned, 35 to 45 minutes. Serve warm.

Zucchini and Squash Tacos
(*Tacos de Calabacitas*)

Adapted from Julian Medina, Chef-Owner, Toloache

TIME: *30 minutes*
YIELD: *4 servings*

2 tablespoons extra-virgin
   olive oil
2 tablespoons minced onion
½ cup diced yellow summer
   squash
½ cup diced zucchini
½ cup corn kernels,
   preferably fresh
1 jalapeño pepper, stemmed,
   seeded, and finely chopped
½ cup diced tomato or
   quartered cherry tomatoes
¼ teaspoon dried oregano
Salt
½ cup grated Monterey Jack
   cheese
8 corn tortillas
1 tablespoon minced cilantro

Julian Medina, the chef and owner of Toloache in Manhattan, found inspiration in a traditional Mexican taco filled with sautéed zucchini and epazote leaves. It was 2009 when he invented his variation with yellow squash, zucchini, tomatoes, and corn, enlivened with onions, jalapeño, and cheese. The result is a taco with fresh, clean, simple flavors that is served straight up—no salsa.

He invented it for his daughter, Olivia, who was 2½ years old in 2009. "She likes zucchini, tomatoes, and corn," said Mr. Medina, who admits that tacos in general are his favorite food. How often does he eat them? At least once a day.

1. In a medium saucepan over medium heat, heat the oil until shimmering. Add the onion and sauté until translucent, about 2 minutes. Add the squash, zucchini, corn kernels, and jalapeño. Sauté until the squash and zucchini are lightly browned, about 3 minutes. Add the tomatoes, oregano, and salt to taste.

2. Cover, reduce the heat to medium-low, and cook, stirring once or twice, until the squash, zucchini, and tomatoes release their juices and begin to blend, 5 to 7 minutes. Uncover, and adjust the salt as needed. Sprinkle with the cheese, cover, and cook until the cheese is melted, about 1 minute. Remove from the heat and keep warm.

{continued}

3. Preheat a griddle or large heavy skillet over medium heat. Working in batches, warm the tortillas on the griddle, about 1 minute a side. Place the warmed tortillas on a platter and cover with foil to keep warm.

4. Arrange 2 warm tortillas on each of four plates. Place equal portions of filling in the center of each tortilla. Garnish with a sprinkling of cilantro and serve.

Zucchini Pancakes

Adapted from Aytekin Yar, Executive Chef, Dardanel

TIME: *30 minutes*
YIELD: *12 pancakes*

FOR THE PANCAKES:

3 medium zucchini, shredded

Salt and freshly ground
   black pepper

3 large eggs, beaten

1/2 cup all-purpose flour

1 tablespoon extra-virgin
   olive oil

1 cup crumbled feta cheese

3 scallions, finely chopped

1/3 cup finely chopped
   fresh dill

1 teaspoon baking powder

4 to 6 tablespoons vegetable
   oil, more as needed

FOR THE YOGURT SAUCE:

2/3 cup plain yogurt

2 garlic cloves, finely chopped

1/2 teaspoon salt

Aytekin Yar, the executive chef at Dardanel on the Upper East Side, eats *mucver*—delicate, crisp zucchini pancakes—at four in the afternoon, before he starts cooking for the dinner crowd.

"I love it because it's tasty, and it's not heavy," Mr. Yar said. His version of *mucver* (pronounced MOOSH-vair) has not just shredded zucchini, but also tiny clouds of feta and a sprinkling of minced fresh dill and scallions. They are crisp on the outside, tender within, and subtly herbaceous.

Mr. Yar was born in Turkey, and his grandmother and mother made the dish a bit differently there. "They fry it, and they chop the pancake and mix it with yogurt," he said. His version is presented as five-inch round pancakes, the garlicky yogurt sauce on the side, but the home cook can make them smaller in diameter.

In Turkey, and in the United States, *mucver* is often eaten as an appetizer. But it can be the centerpiece of a meal, with a salad of sliced tomatoes lightly dressed with oil and vinegar on the side.

The trick to making the pancakes crisp and not soggy is to squeeze all the water out of the zucchini before mixing it with the other ingredients. A little brute force is required.

1. Preheat the oven to 250°F. Place the zucchini in a colander over a bowl and mix with 1/2 teaspoon salt. Allow to drain for 5 minutes. Transfer to a cloth kitchen towel and squeeze hard to extract as much

{continued}

moisture as possible. Squeeze a second time; the volume will shrink to about half the original.

2. In a large mixing bowl, combine the zucchini and eggs. Using a fork, mix well. Add the flour, $\frac{1}{2}$ teaspoon salt, the olive oil, feta, scallions, dill, and $\frac{1}{2}$ teaspoon black pepper. Mix well, add the baking powder, and mix again.

3. Place a cast-iron skillet or other heavy skillet over medium heat. Add 2 tablespoons vegetable oil and heat until shimmering. Place heaping tablespoons of the zucchini batter in the pan several inches apart, allowing room to spread. Flatten them with a spatula, if necessary; the pancakes should be about $\frac{3}{8}$ inch thick and about 3 inches in diameter. Fry until golden on one side, then turn and fry again until golden on the other side. Repeat once or twice, frying about 5 to 6 minutes total, so the pancakes get quite crisp. Transfer to a plate lined with paper towels and keep warm in the oven. Continue frying the remaining batter, adding more oil to the pan as needed. Serve hot.

4. For the yogurt sauce: In a small bowl, combine the yogurt, garlic, and salt. Mix well, and serve on the side or on the pancakes.

Acknowledgments

I want to thank all the chefs and cooks who so generously shared and demonstrated their delicious recipes with me. They prove that vegetarianism is not only delectable, but also exciting.

I'd like to thank everyone at the *New York Times* who made possible first the column, and then the book. Thanks go to Pete Wells, the editor of the Dining Section who first launched the column, and to Trish Hall, the editor of our department (Home, Dining, Real Estate, Styles), for watching over the column to the end, approving recipes, and editing the final batch of introductions, all with a deft, light hand. Other editors also applied their surgical talents to the text: Pat Gurosky, Jonathan Paul, and Nick Fox. Emily Weinstein, our Web wizard, posted each weekly column with flair on the *Times'* Web site.

Some colleagues had tasty tips. Julia Moskin, a reporter, said go to Tamarind Tribeca and eat the saag with the Tater Tots (they turned out to be little fried potato balls), and give a call to Ayinde Howell, a vegan chef. Nikki Kalish, an art director, said to call Roland Caracostea, a graphic designer, for his spectacular endive tart. John Hyland touted Raffaela Ronca at Palma. Those were very bright ideas. Thanks, too, to Linda Conte, for ongoing, cheerful helpfulness.

In New Hampshire, reachable by e-mail, thanks to Denise Landis, who edited the recipes with great thoughtfulness and care.

I want to thank Julia Chang Bloch, my oldest friend, who wrote "Chinese Home Cooking" with me for the Organization of Chinese American Women in 1985. A few of the recipes are in this book.

Special thanks go to Leslie Wells, the executive editor at Hyperion, who asked if the column could become a book. Alex Ward, at the *Times*, said yes, as did my agent, Angela Miller. Karen Minster created a handsome design for the book.

Last, I thank my vegetarian daughter, Anna, who, each Sunday night, invited friends over for a tasting dinner. As I cooked my way through the recipes, they ate and kibitzed. More lemon? Pass the salt, please. Mmmmmm.

Elaine Louie is a staff member of the *New York Times*, where she writes the "Temporary Vegetarian" column for the Diners Journal blog online, and also contributes to the Home and Style sections. Louie won the 1995 James Beard Journalism Award, and is author or co-author of eleven other books on entertaining, design, and fashion. She lives in Manhattan.

Index

W

Y